Anastasiya Malynka

UX design essential handbook

Beginner to Junior UX Designer

Contents

How it started

Nobody can be a Pro on the first try; no one can rush into something new and make it great without preparation.

When I started in IT, UX as a job was so weird for me. I remember how I was checking out the positions on the market and couldn't wrap my head around how it was even possible to work as a UX when everyone was expected to ensure "the best quality and experience" for the users, no matter if you're a Junior or Senior designer.

What even was that "best quality"? My technical brain wanted an exact definition, formula, or set of parameters defining the expected successful result. For me, Design, as a term, was around appearance, graphics, and how everything worked, not the "quality" and "functionality." That's why in my head the was no space for UX for a while. "QA for quality, developers for the functionality, and designers for the appearance," that's what I was thinking, "Why would there be any other role? How many more specialists would we need to make a good, well-built, competitive product? Why are we keep stacking up the positions that overlap and mix and match the responsibility instead of just getting things done?" But that was due to a lack of proper research and not a very developed market for UX specialists at that time. A few years later, I gave it another try and went through a good Book on product design, not even UX specifically. Little by little, piece by piece, I was collecting information about the industry, definitions, understanding concepts, and building my Vision. And finally, at some point, I realized that I wanted to be a Pro in UX.

Nowadays, when it looks like every "expert" has a blog on Medium or answers you on Reddit, why would you read a 200-pages book? We have too much content: videos, podcasts, personal and company blogs, educational websites and games, and online courses. Everyone strives to optimize their educational time and wants to get new knowledge and profession as quickly as possible, ideally in an hour, maybe less, without much work and effort but with outstanding achievements and compensation. I am just kidding. And I'm not being mean; I'm not the exception either. Please give me everything prepared and ready to consume! A new profession in 5 days? I'm up to it! New business in 30 days? Come on, let's do it! But also, I'm a person who trusts in self-education. And even though I have two degrees, I entirely admit that the primary skills I use daily for business and personal arrangements are self-taught.

For me, that Book was a crucial element to understanding the sphere; it gave me the base and helped define a correct structure before I went into all-wild and read hundreds of blogs.

No, for sure, it wasn't just one book. I collected information from many resources to really understand design, usability, business, and strategy.

No, I'm not saying to ditch the blogs and the internet; books are not perfect either. But compared to hundreds and thousands of opinions that can be reflected in personal blogs online, I trust books more, at least because a typical book is written in 4 to 8 months, based on experience combined with research and analysis, whereas a blog post in 2 to 8 hours. Time is not the key, but Effort is.

Like many of us, long before I tried to use some of the skills and methods I learned, I was going through pages and pages of materials, making my own "database" of theory. "Database" in this case is a stack of information about terms, definitions, activities, methods, literally anything connected to the topic I learned about. The path was built through books, articles written by famous and experienced specialists, case studies, and other valuable materials. The "database" might sound serious and complicated, but, in reality, at least for the first 2-3 years of my journey in UX, due to me being a visual learner, it was just a vast A4 dotted journal. And when I started working in the new role, I gradually expanded my database, not only with new topics but also covering tips and personal findings, making my version of the "Half-Blood Prince book" for that "database".

Based on my initial database, I grew in my role in UX, mentored more than a hundred mentees, completed several dozens of products, and wrote a few educational programs. Currently, it's not just a journal anymore but an extensive system of digital and physical notes. I use it whenever I need to review theories, prepare for an interview, or find the answers. That's a great practice that helped me. Therefore, I encourage my students to develop their own "databases."

In this handbook, I'm sharing the first part of my notes and materials for levels A0-A1 or Beginner to Junior UX Designers.

I will never present it as "one single source of truth". I will encourage you to read and learn more about each of the covered topics, but that's definitely will be the steady base, which will help you to start a career in UX design. That will inspire and, also, engage you in some of the primary and more advanced activities. The handbook is not meant to be one and only one source, but it will help you to get brief and straight-to-the-point information - a step-by-step process, and prepare you for the technical or project interview.

Only about 1% of the companies, digital, and tech giants use and cherish UX. Not only as a role or position, or fancy title but as an approach and a way of addressing problems. The boom in demand for UX specialists is highly connected to the specifics of our sphere. On the one hand, because of market preferences: many companies don't need UX as an essential role. Still, they manage to use it as a cover for the universal unicorn position that mixes Graphic, UI, UX, Web, and other similar expertise, including the word "Design". On the other hand, every year, more and more companies realize the fundamental role and power of UX, and due to high competition in the market, strive for it on the same level as used to seek good SEO and marketing.

The UX-like term is not only about design itself; it can be focused on UX research, UX writing, or hated by me term UX/UI, or any other Unicorn position you can find. But for me, it's not about the work or title, but about the activities and value, you bring to the team. This handbook is built to maximize your learning path and give a steady base for anyone who feels inspired and motivated to start and boost their career as a self-taught designer.

Every year the entry-level UX, as for any specialty, grows. What was "nice to have" even 2-3 years ago, is a "must have" now, so in the book are included not only basic materials, but some intermediate and even a few advanced topics for you to really stand out. The last section of this book is focused on portfolios and interviews. I've included a few tips from my experience as a candidate and technical interviewer, and hope they will help you as well.

Being a self-taught UX designer is possible, not always easy, but definitely doable. Study the basics, practice the activities, understand the process, do a few educational or volunteering projects in UX and take care of your portfolio and CV. So if you are ready to start this journey and get a new career or boost your basic knowledge, this handbook is here for you and I say "You got it".

How to use the handbook

The handbook is built based on the classic design process and framework of Double Diamond, so all of the activities have a logical connection to the typical process. The overall structure is split into 12 modules and covers more than 130 items in 90+ topics that you might encounter in the Junior designer position. Besides that, significant activities and some extras to enhance your design toolkit will be covered in this handbook.

My goal was to reflect terms and methods in the handbook the same way I would for my "database" journal; I call it the 3S method: *Simple*, *Straightforward*, and *Strategic*.

Simple: We say "No" to theoretical jargon and long pages for methods that can not be explained painlessly.

Straightforward: We say "No" to complicated definitions and use samples, tips, and visualization where applicable to ensure that information is well-presented and can be reviewed or digested quickly.

Strategic: We say "No" to using activities and methods only to enrich the portfolio or because we are taught to. We want to understand the motivation and reasoning behind our actions, what we are doing, when, and what is expected. And this is what defines a good specialist! Not every project requires the Persona, not every time we need wireframes, and we shouldn't include them just for because.

Use this handbook as a "database" journal, grab a pen to make notes, add extras, or have a spare notebook on a side to create your own "database." Review it before interviews, when working on the project, or starting in a new role. Mark the topics needing extra info, and expand your knowledge by reviewing domain-specific books and articles from other authors. This handbook covers all the basics so you can start your journey without any UX or IT experience.

Illustration 0: Original "database" of mine

Disclaimer

Even though this book is focused on UX activities and covers research, usability, design process and principles, it also includes basic UI modules to highlight importance of UI in UX design.

Remember: there is UI without UX and many cases it's a usability disaster, but there is not good UX without UI, so it's your responsibility to always work on it. UX is a skill, that should be obtained, trained and enhanced, but UI is a muscle, you can't read a book and be good in UI, practice makes the difference.

Good luck!

Module 1: UX in the design

Topic 1.1: UX or UI

UX is a relatively new definition that became popular in the 20th century after Don Norman performed in Apple as the first designer with UX in his title. But the fact that the term UX is relatively new doesn't mean that the craft of User Experience was created recently. The prerequisites for the emergence of UX began to appear long before our era. People cared about their living spaces and improved them with ergonomics, wanted to improve the work environments, created systems to enhance and optimize the work process, and many more.

Here are a few historical cases directly related to UX:

1) In the 1940s, S. Toyota began to use the "5 Whys" technique in developing cars and introduced its use in factories to determine the root cause of problems, which is solved with the user in mind. It formed the basis of human-oriented design. In the same period, they started the first usability tests with an orientation toward the end user.

2) In the 1950s, Disney entered the theme park industry. The innovator envisioned the park as an immersive experience where every detail is considered. His team received management principles later known as "Mickey's 10 Commandments". These ten principles are very similar to the UX design principles used today.

3) In 1993, Don Norman joined Apple as a user experience architect, making him the first person to have "UX" in his job title. It was he who invented the term "user experience." Norman was the first person to coin the phrase "UX" and "user-centered design" and earned the status of "Father

of UX." As a result of his involvement, Apple is widely recognized as a leader in UX design.

Were they specifically UX specialists? No, probably, except Don Norman. But did they care about the Experience? Sure, they did! Let's understand the difference between User Interface Design (UXD), User Interface Design (UI), and Interaction Design (IDX).

UXD

User Experience design — interaction with the user — is about exchanging the interface with the user. UX follows the user's journey when interacting with a product or service. Experience design is creating products and services that provide a meaningful user experience, involving many different areas of product development, including branding, usability, functionality, and overall "design." A functional product is not enough; it must be attractive, convenient, and serviceable to be competitive in the market. Let's consider the design experience from a process perspective. It is anchored in research, planning, analysis, and other activities, including testing, and works more closely with the end user.

UID

User interface design is the space of interaction between humans and machines. The user interface is an integral aspect of interaction with it, which consists of 2 main parts:
- a visible design that conveys the appearance of the product,
- an interaction design is a functional and logical organization of elements.

The UI design method creates an interface that facilitates interaction and creates an efficient and pleasant environment for users who interact with the product. The stages of developing a UI will be visual research, building components, and forming a visual layout of the page. UX and UI design go hand in hand and interact.

IxD

Interaction design is the design of interactive products and services in which the designer focuses beyond elements or layouts to how users interact. Thus, careful analysis of user needs, constraints, and context allows the designer to achieve productive outcomes according to precise requirements. Interaction design addresses general interaction issues and how the interface elements interact with the user and each other.

Five levels can be applied in interaction design:
- Words,
- Visible representation or presentation of graphic elements,
- Physical objects and space,
- Time,
- Behavior.

In many companies, employees are T-shaped, with key specializations and additional skills, so different meanings can be attached to the role. So typically, we cannot define UX design with UI, as in many cases, UI represents the UX solutions and principles. Interestingly enough, this does not apply to UI. We can have almost pure UI, but in most cases, it will practically become the Graphic design, as it won't fulfill the requirements, and usability standards and won't be usable enough, which means the product has a huge chance of becoming not helpful and not wanted by users.

Topic 1.2: Why do we care about UX

Design, as a matter of quality, can impact our product positively or negatively. Sometimes it takes a great effort to move the product higher based on the usability and UX perspective.

UX design:

- Makes a solid first impression. Good design is a harmonious, balanced use of color, shape, texture, space, image, and content.
- It drives users to action. The professional design takes into account both end users and business.
- Makes product use simple.
- Promotes development in social networks. Social media is one of the best ways to attract customers, go viral, and make a name for your business.

What is "good design"? Dieter Rams said that it should be:

- Innovative
- Makes the product useful
- Aesthetic
- Makes the product understandable
- Unobtrusive
- Honest
- Lasting
- Consistent with the last detail
- Eco-friendly
- Includes as little design as possible

Good design is a complex question. It makes the product more accessible and comfortable, but it's not just about looking good. A design must perform a specific function to be "beautiful" and practical. Good design is how something looks and works. Design can improve interaction or usability reputation. There is no single understanding of "good" or "bad" design, but there are guidelines and rules in UX that can help you achieve better results.

Topic 1.3: Usable or Useful design

The basic understanding of the UX is typically built around the terms Usable and Useful. We use them to define the main characteristics of the product.

Usable defines the product's usability or if it's easy to use. We check how the product is used, whether it is pleasant, simple, practical, functional, or logical.

Useful defines the usefulness of the product. A useful product enables the user to accomplish a task or goal. While in many contexts, these tasks are clear and measurable, in other contexts, they may not be.

But usable and valuable are not the only factors, and even if the product is comfortable, pleasant and functional, or both useful and usable, it still cannot be **used**. Without users, the product is a failure, and it doesn't matter how great the design is; it's still a failure. Therefore, before starting any product development, we investigate the market. The user needs to ensure that the proposed solution is required, the product is competitive, and the "quality + pricing" combination is desirable by potential users.

Topic 1.4: UX role in user advocacy

It is often heard that a UX designer advocates for the user, but when creating a product, we take into account the views of the business, the user, and the technical capabilities.

> User needs are not equal to business needs.
> An unhappy user **is** a business problem.
> An unhappy business **is not** the user's problem.

User advocacy on the project can take different forms:
- User engagement. Testers and actual users have other intentions and mindsets: the former to test the product, the latter to use it. It is almost impossible to simulate the real personal needs of users.
- Investment inaccurate user data, not guesswork. When involving users at all stages of research, be prepared that any of your assumptions may be disproved.
- Minimization of bias. To minimize it, you need to either involve people outside the project to objectively evaluate the product or rely on teams of external users.
- They are balancing needs. What we can develop is not always what the user needs and not always what the user wants - actually needs. Communicate the decision and its potential impact on each party.

You need to understand business opportunities and needs, know what the user wants and needs, see the roadmap, and predict results.

It is worth remembering that a UX designer does not work in a vacuum of ideas and research, so sometimes, the opinion of the business or its needs become no less important; they need to be balanced.

Module 2: UX in product development

Topic 2.1: SDLC and the role of design in it

The concept of **SDLC describes the software development life cycle** and a practical methodology with well-defined processes for creating high-quality software.

A typical SDLC consists of 6 stages, they are adaptable and can be changed depending on the specifics of the product, and the process that sometimes is unique to the team.

1) Analysis

2) Planning

3) Design

4) Development

5) Testing

6) Deployment

Before starting work, you need to understand what will be created and find out what is already on the market and what is ahead. In the **Analysis** stage, we look for gaps we can fill as a business or product. During the analysis phase, we usually learn the basic requirements, the environment in which our product will be used, the constraints, and the goals. The next stage is **Planning**. At this stage, we need to decide our ultimate goal, what exactly needs to be done to achieve it, where we will start, and how we will allocate resources: time and money. The third stage is **Design**. Design at this stage is not only prototyping; it is usually a more general concept that describes low-level components, algorithms, architecture creation, UI development, technical design creation, and more. The fourth stage is **Development**. After designing and planning, the actual writing of the code that will perform a specific task and achieve the expected results takes place. After that, **Testing** is expected. Testing involves finding flaws and ways to improve and working through cases. During the testing phase, we expect the product to be "up to specification" or at an objective level of quality before it can be presented to users. And the last logical stage will be the stage of deployment or release. We can apply the changes when testing is complete and make the product available to customers. The SDLC cycle is not always linear and depends on the framework or process used; some stages may be repetitive or iterative.

A **framework** is a solution infrastructure that facilitates the development of complex systems, that is, a specific template or format that helps systematize processes. "Iterative" refers to the repeatability of a particular operation or phase to achieve system improvement. Sometimes interactivity means that a specific task is performed several times and implies that the study's results may not always be successful. However, iterations are an essential part of any agile development process.

Depending on the framework, UX design can be embedded in different stages, focusing on the Research and Design activities. Therefore the role of the UX designer is quite diverse, and, depending on the company, the type of product can be cyclically focused on a particular stage or distributed over all phases of the SDLC.

Tasks of a UX designer at different stages of the SDLC

Stage	Tasks
Analysis	- Collection and analysis of requirements - Interviews with customers and users - Competitors analysis - Other studies
Planning	- UX planning - Defining of scope - Estimation and Prioritization - Creating a product roadmap
Design	- Ideation and generation of ideas - Creating a design system - Creating patterns and components - Graphic Design - User Interface design - Initial testing with users
Development	- FE support - Creation of design documentation
Testing	- UI and usability testing - Creation of guides for users
Deployment	- Work with documentation - Feedback collection - Improvement planning

Topic 2.2: Agile vs. Waterfall

Various frameworks are used when creating a product; they can be classic or adjusted by each team.

The four most popular frameworks are:

- Waterfall is a linear framework,
- Agile is a flexible framework,
- The V-model is an iterative framework,
- The spiral model is a cyclical framework.

Waterfall

Describes a step-by-step approach to developing a project with an established set of actions and activities. This means you start with requirements gathering and documenting data, then move on to design, development, testing, deployment, and delivery. A subsequent stage can begin if the current phase is completed, and the result is the culmination of all the steps involved in producing the final product. The Waterfall is very simple in its general sense and unequivocal, but also it makes it limited, inflexible, and unfortunately unpredictable.

Agile

A flexible methodology that replaces rigid structures with a more collaborative process where requirements and deliverables evolve through iterations, with an emphasis on teamwork.

With Agile methodology, a project team can establish a few initial requirements and proceed to design, development, testing, and deployment. After deployment, the team collects feedback and sets new conditions for the next update. This cycle continues until the final desired product is achieved. Agile is much more flexible, quick, and involves a multifunctional team, but also less predictable due to less documentation and often followed by frequent changes.

Topic 2.3: Scrum, Kanban, and Lean

Agile methodologies can be implemented through Scrum and Kanban frameworks and the Lean philosophy.

Scrum

This framework allows you to implement the Agile development methodology. Unlike the waterfall model, Scrum provides an iterative and gradual development process. The project is divided into several stages, the result of each of which is a ready-to-use product. A usable product or sub-module is delivered to the customer at the end of each step, called a sprint in Scrum terminology. A typical team consists of a PO, a Scrum Master, and the Scrum Team.

Kanban

Kanban is a visual system for managing work in the format of actual tasks. Kanban aims to identify potential bottlenecks and problem points in your process and eliminate them so that work can flow through it cost-effectively at optimal speed and throughput. A Kanban board with tasks in different states is usually used. Generally, each team member can work on up to two tasks simultaneously.

Lean

Lean is a concept that emphasizes the optimization of efficiency and minimization of waste in the development process of a product or software.

Lean is formed on seven main principles:

- Waste disposal.
- Build quality.
- Improving learning.
- Postponing commitments as long as possible.
- Fast results.
- Respect for people.
- Optimization of everything.

Topic 2.4: UX without process

When it comes to standardization or description of processes, you need to understand that the most significant value of such formalization is convenience, which is directly proportional to the type of project and the number of team members. If we are talking about a small project and a team of 3-5 people, a mini-startup, we understand that processes are more of a recommendation than a need. But typical processes become necessary if it is a larger project, with a team of 10-20 people or even more.

The process helps standardize activities, avoid conflicts, and improve the delivery process. All team members will understand what, when, and why they need to do it, how to frame the results, and make the overall work more transparent, which is essential for many customers.

The defined process brings:

- **Unambiguousness.** The team does not guess and interpret them according to the situation "today." All participants clearly understand the details.
- **Motivation and concentration.** Just as uniforms take the pain out of choosing when you're going to work, understanding processes helps you plan tasks and resources.
- **More expected result.** No one forbids working ad-hoc, but the well-thought-out process and at least minimal reporting make it possible to predict the probable outcome.
- **Better communication with the customer.** Many people need to be aware and want to understand when they will get specific results. After all, most customers do not know what happens to obtain these "results."

The role of a UX designer is not static and is not limited to creating layouts or icons. This is a dynamic process with tasks at different stages of work on the project. With a defined process, it is easier to synchronize team actions. This affects the outcome, quality, and timing of the task.

Topic 2.5: Design Thinking

The design thinking process is a human-centered problem-solving approach with a primary emphasis on empathy to identify deep needs and target users, creating an alternative way of thinking when considering possible solutions.

Typically, the process is carried out in 5 or 6 (if we take into account the implementation) stages of design development:

1. Empathize
2. Define
3. Ideate
4. Prototype
5. Test

Empathize

At this stage, we want to enhance our understanding of user and compassion. We ask:

- Who is the user?
- What is essential to this person?
- How does this feature fit into their lives?
- What motivates or discourages users?
- Where do they feel frustrated?

Typically, we can conduct user interviews, create personas, investigate and create customer journey maps, do various workshops like 5W(H), or work directly with empathy maps.

Define

At this stage, we want to define the problem and find all the constraints, pain points, or other issues that may limit our users. We ask:

- What problem is this object trying to solve?
- What do we want to achieve?
- How do we see ourselves, have we succeeded?

We could start with a brief description of the project in any briefing exercise, define our goals, test with users' existing experience (assess problem points), conduct interviews with interested parties, and define KPIs.

Ideation

This stage is all about generating ideas and finding solutions. We ask:
- What ideas can we bring?
- What solutions are valuable?

We are conducting brainstorming, competitive, and comparative analysis, body storming, various ideation activities, creating mental maps, and sketching.

Prototype

After we have many ideas, we need to work them out and understand if they are precious and if they are solving our problem. We ask:
- How can pictures be presented?
- What do you need to build for user testing?

Typically, work involves creating digital wireframes, physical prototypes, rapid prototyping, and other activities.

Test

And finally, we are testing our solution. We ask:
- What are users telling us that we can fix?
- What went well?
- Where are users experiencing difficulties?

There are many testing activities, starting from guerrilla testing to work with usability testing, heuristics, analytics, and more.

Why is design thinking popular?

- It revolves around a deep interest in understanding the people for whom we develop products and services.
- It helps us observe and develop empathy for target users.
- Improves our ability to ask questions: you question the problem, assumptions, and clues.
- It is beneficial when solving problems that need to be better defined or known.
- Involves constant experimentation through sketching, prototyping, testing, and testing new concepts and ideas.

Design thinking is an iterative process where you seek to understand your users, challenge assumptions, rethink problems, and create innovative solutions that can be prototyped and tested.

Topic 2.6: Human-centered design

Human-centered design is a problem-solving technique that puts real people at the center of the design process, allowing you to create products and services that resonate with and adapt to the needs of your audience. The goal is to keep users' desires, concerns, and preferences in mind at every process stage. In turn, you'll create more intuitive, accessible products that will likely be more profitable because your customers have already tested the solution and feel more invested in its implementation.

The process is built on three stages: **inspiration, idea, and implementation** (illustration 1). Sometimes implementation is called delivery, and motivation is called understanding or empathy.

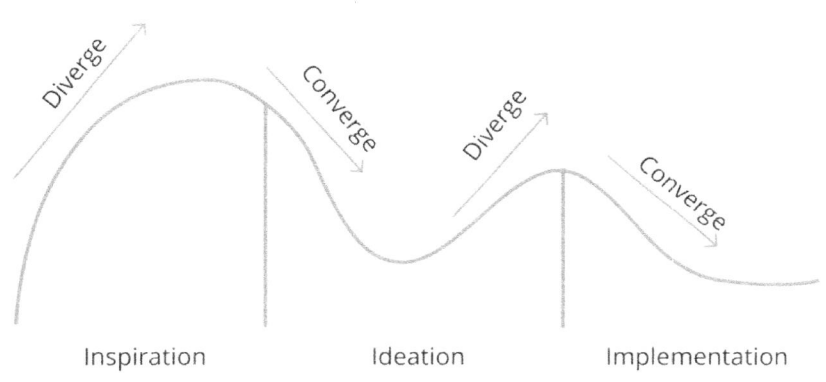

Illustration 1: 3 stages of HCD

How to adhere to HCD?
- Consider this design process as a team "sport," being human-oriented in decisions is not only about designers and creatives; it is about research and involvement of many other specialists, from analysts to marketing.
- Make user feedback routine; it should not be an additional unplanned expense once every six months but a constant iterative process.
- You are not a user: talk to them, conduct a field study, look for answers, and not focus on the most apparent solutions;
- Build MVP prototypes, and test.

Topic 2.7: Double Diamond

Double Diamond is one of the project's classic models of the design process. The Double Diamond design pattern has been around since the British Design Council officially invented it in 2005. The official Double Diamond design model has four stages: Discover, Define, Develop and Deliver (illustration 2). Together, these stages work as a map designers can use to organize their thoughts and ideas and improve the creative process.

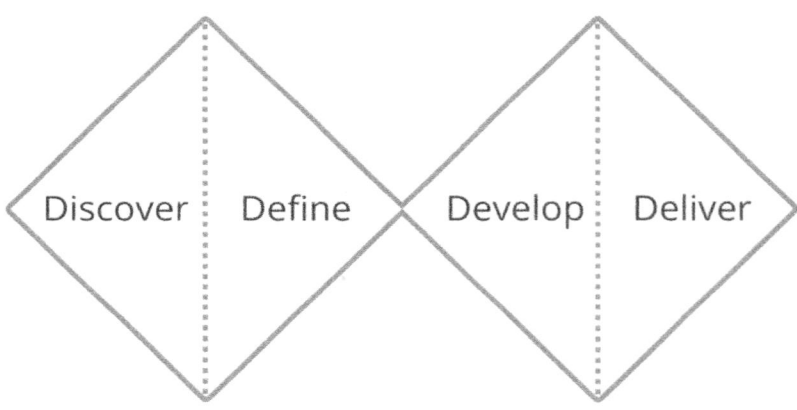

Illustration 2: 4 stages of Double Diamond

Discover: data collection

This stage is about learning more about the various variables that affect the problem and its possible solution. Companies typically begin this process by articulating their problem, presenting their hypothesis, and identifying ways to learn more. This stage aims to identify and contextualize the actual situation or the possibility of its solution.

Define: data filtering and analysis

It consists of filtering all the information you receive at the first stage and processing it in detail. This can mean identifying bottlenecks or waste of resources, uncovering hidden opportunities, or establishing a list of things the design team absolutely must not do (so-called no-gos).

Develop: design of the product

This is a broader design concept, including UX and UI design, technical design, and architecture; in other words, it is the "realization" or the actual product creation. The development phase involves much interdisciplinary work - bringing designers together with internal partners such as engineers, developers, or other departments with the expertise needed for the project. A significant advantage of this development stage is that you speed up the problem-solving process by bringing different departments together.

Deliver: test and release

Final testing is being done to take one last look at the product version and ensure there are no issues. Includes testing for compliance with regulations and legal standards, damage testing, and compatibility testing.

Advantages of the Double diamond approach:

- A simplified development model that covers most of the necessary stages and is light enough not to complicate the process.
- An iterative approach in this process allows you to work out likely solutions and quickly adapt.
- Is built on user interaction and testing principles, which makes its philosophy close to HCD.

Double diamond is flexible and involves iterability, like other models.

Topic 2.8: Types of UX awareness

Project management theory defines four stages of project maturity:
- Introduction — an entry when the product is just entering the market.
- Growth is when the product gathers its primary audience and develops.
- Maturity is when the product is at the peak of its popularity.
- The decline is a stage when a product becomes irrelevant.

Understanding the stage of product development allows us to understand approaches to process design at different stages of maturity. And also look from a certain angle at the UXD stage of development of organizations that are similar in a certain way but do not have a point of decline.

UX unaware

Companies that don't know about UX at all. At this level, product functionality is considered the most important. When user experience is assumed, visual design often needs to clarify it. It is not only about failure to perform classic UX activities but also about inconsistency in the design process.

Random UX or ad-hoc

The start of awareness within an organization usually comes when someone in management attends a conference and learns about UX or a specific employee tries to gain organizational support by demonstrating the value of UX to the organization.

Companies try to implement UX on their own or hire a consultant. Either approach is unlikely to be effective because the organization needs to gain the skills and experience to integrate UX into its existing process successfully.

Projects with a focus on UX

The point at which UX can become a permanent component of the development process. The level at which UX can be strategically positioned.

Analytics and product planning are used on an ongoing basis. Leaders and teams are rewarded for meeting UX goals. The organization sees the value of UX and decides that it should be consistently integrated into projects. Some forms of formal process and documentation of UX activities are introduced.

An organization with a focus on UX

UX in the projects of such a company takes place at the organizational level. Here, UX is considered not separate tasks but project processes that affect people and products.

Projects developed at the level of one business context have a standard or consistent UX value system. The "discovery" process is widely used for analyzing the work process and the product and for internal users.

The role of the UX designer in the project depends not only on the distribution of roles in the team and the accepted design process model. The stages of UX development in the organization also affect your responsibilities and position.

Module 3: UX planning and work with requirements

Topic 3.1: Requirements

Requirements are the rules, vision, and functional description that explain how the system should work and look. Analyzing customer requirements is a critical process that allows you to evaluate the success of a system or software project. Requirements are usually divided into two types: Functional requirements and Non-functional requirements.

Functional

The requirements the end user explicitly requires are the essential capabilities the system should offer. All these functions must be included in the system as part of the contract. They are presented or formulated as input data that must be provided to the system regarding the operation performed and the expected result. These are user-stated requirements that can be seen directly in the final product instead of non-functional requirements.

Attributes of functional requirement:

- Defines a system or its component.
- Describes, "What should a software system do?"
- Specified by the user.
- Is mandatory.

- Applied in a concrete use case or refers to a particular flow of user interaction with the product.
- Helps test software functionality.
- Usually easily determined.

Examples:

1) "User authentication must occur every time he/she logs into the system."

2) "A confirmation email is sent to the user every time he/she first registers on the system."

Non-functional

The system must meet the quality constraints according to the project contract. The priority or degree of implementation of these factors varies from project to project. They are also called non-behavioral requirements.

They mainly deal with such issues as:
- Portability
- Security
- Reliability
- Scalability
- Productivity

Attributes of functional requirement:
- Defines the quality attribute of the software system.
- Imposes constraints on "How must a software system meet the requirements?"
- Specified by technical people, for example, an Architect.
- Is not mandatory.
- Applies to the system as a whole.
- Helps to test software performance.

- Is usually more challenging to determine.

Examples:

1) "Emails should be sent with a delay of no more than 12 hours after a specific action."

2) "Each request must be processed within 10 seconds."

Understanding functional and non-functional requirements gives the designer more approaches and tactics for decision-making.

Topic 3.2: BRD and FRD

Regarding requirements, it is worth defining the types of conditions documentation you may encounter on the project. There can be quite a lot of such documents containing information about the requirements, but the difference is that:

- Who creates them?
- What level of information is available in these documents?
- At what stage are these documents created?
- Who uses these documents?
- What is the purpose of the document?

BRD

A Business Requirements Document (BRD) is a formal document that defines the goals and expectations an organization hopes to achieve by working with a supplier to complete a specific project.

BRD deals with what the organization hopes to achieve through partnering with the performer.

In BRD, typically included:

- General goal(s) of the project.
- A high-level description of what the project should achieve, for example, what niche we want to occupy in the market or how many users to gather and at what time.
- How the goal supports larger strategic goals.
- List of involved stakeholders.
- The background of the project (how it came about and the problems or opportunities that arose).
- Business factors that make this project necessary (operational, market, environmental or financial).
- Description of current and proposed processes (diagrams may be included).

FRD

A Functional Requirements Document (FRD) is a formal document that details the requirements to achieve business needs. The copy serves the purpose of the contract so that the customer can agree on what they consider acceptable for the product's capabilities. The functional requirements document is the primary document for product development.

The functional requirements specified in the document define the system's expected behavior. FRD describes the expected result and behavior that can be implemented as tasks, services, or functions.

In FRD typically included:

- Project description – a brief overview of the project contains information about the prerequisites or conditions that created the need for the product.
- Description of the audience and potential market.
- Contact persons.
- Links to documents.

- Data requirements.
- Process requirements.

A business requirements document (BRD) describes the high-level business needs, while a functional requirements document (FRD) describes the functions required to meet the business needs.

BRD answers what the business wants to do, while FRD answers how it should be done. **FRD is derived from BRD.**

Topic 3.3: 3 main constraints

In the theory of product management, there is the concept of the Iron Triangle. The Iron Triangle defines that product development works within three design constraints: **budget, time, and tasks**. Depending on the project or who is involved, each of these limitations may be the most important to the end user. These are not the only constraints you might have, but they are the base for all others.

It is necessary to balance the possibilities within these three constraints to succeed.

Cost/budget

Cost is the financial constraint of the iron triangle, also called the budget. Project costs can include various elements, including resources such as materials, people, funds, and anything else that affects the project.

In some cases, costs are fixed and cannot change. In others, prices are variable and can be adjusted according to needs and capabilities.

Time

The iron triangle's time limit means the project's planned completion. Time management is closely related to task management, as the overall schedule is divided into individual tasks and expected completion times. To manage time, project managers must identify tasks that need to be completed in sequence and are interdependent.

Quality

In the project triangle, the scope includes the tasks required to achieve the project's goals and the expected level of quality for each module as a whole. Controlling the area of project tasks is particularly critical because scope adjustments almost always affect cost and time. Incorrect execution of functions leads to rework and affects cost and time.

These three elements are interconnected (illustration 3). It takes work to achieve all three at once. In most projects, the team sacrifices quality, money, or time.

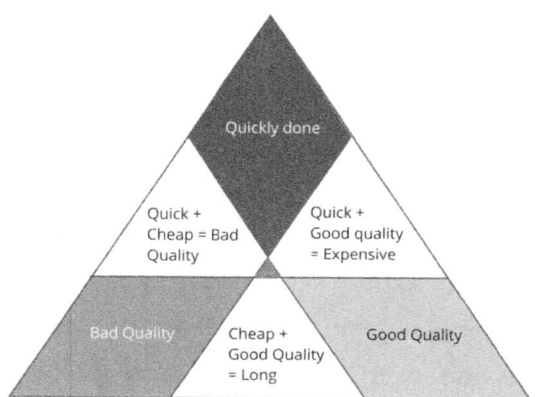

Illustration 3: Iron Triangle in Design

When starting a project, a designer must understand what is most important for the client to build communication with him properly.

Topic 3.4: Kick-off meeting

Kick-off, or project start meeting, is the first introductory meeting with the project team and the client, where possible. This meeting is a time to establish common goals and the project's purpose. Since this is the first meeting between project team members and the client or sponsor, it is the best time to set expectations and build strong team morale.

Usually, the work begins after completing the job description or project brief, and all parties are ready to work.

Kick-off meeting structure:
- Introduction (greetings).
- Questions about the history and motivation of the project.
  Why is development initiated?
  Expected results? Ask about the client's vision.
- Scope of the project and terms.
- Budgets or restrictions can be discussed if needed.
- Roles and responsibilities.
- Process.

To prepare

1) Make a list of points you expect to close during the kick-off (questions, theses, open ends of contact).
2) Select the team present at the meeting and assign the roles.
3) Identify a facilitator.

4) Make a detailed meeting plan, and write down questions and details that are mandatory for discussion.

5) Include a break in the timing and plan activities so they stay within 2 hours.

6) Choose a time and place (it can be an offline or online meeting).

7) Prepare your materials (presentation, notebooks, plan, etc.).

A facilitator is a person who plans, directs, and manages a group event to achieve its goals. Usually, the facilitator is a team member, but there may be cases when an invited person acts as a facilitator.

During the meeting

1) Introduce yourself and the team.

2) Communicate the plan for the meeting and the time constraints you have.

3) Let the client explain his/her vision of the project or the purpose of its creation.

4) Ask questions about your plan and ensure the person responsible for the recording is doing it.

5) Once you've asked all the key questions and discussed the necessary details, consult the next steps.

6) Arrange the next meeting or further cooperation.

After the meeting

1) Send all participants a follow-up with the results and summary of the meeting. Include the next steps there and describe the arrangements you had.

2) Clarify disputed points or send additional materials by email.

3) Remind stakeholders of any other essential materials or documents they need to provide on their part.

4) Analyze the results.

5) The format of the follow-up letter can be pretty accessible, but it is recommended to include the following points:

- *Subject:* "Kick-off meeting follow up" you can also add a date, project name, or other tags to help stakeholders pay attention to your email.

- *Greetings:* This section is used to thank stakeholders for attending the meeting.

- *Body:* Include a brief description of what happened during the meeting, including binding agreements and details (e.g., the scope of work, timeline, the team involved, tasks, vision, etc.).

- *Action items:* Plan next steps for both group and stakeholders (e.g., "Send document A by July 5th", "Schedule a meeting on July 7th", etc., here be specific).

- *Closing:* In this part, you can remind the stakeholder of upcoming scheduled meetings or ask her to confirm the accuracy of the letter above.

After holding the kick-off meeting and formulating the brief, you are ready to proceed to the next stage - project planning.

Topic 3.5: Design Brief

A Design Brief, sometimes called a design specification, is a project management document that outlines its specifics.

There are many reasons to use a project assignment, but two are the most important: efficiency and focus.

Who can write a design brief?

- Designer
- Design head or team leader
- Business analyst

or

- Representative of the customer
- Customer

The design brief can either be provided to the designer for processing or created at the beginning of the project.

Usually, a brief is created:

- Before starting the project.
- After determining the basic requirements.
- After establishing an initial agreement, it can be updated up till the moment when the team starts working on the project.

It helps to build an initial line of understanding and ensure that all parties understand the task at hand and the initial requirements at the same level. Typically, the structure of the brief can be flexible. The key is to record the project's basic information, tasks, and wishes or limitations.

The design brief may include the following:

- Business overview
- Project overview and scope
- Information about the target audience
- Information about competitors
- Project goals
- Project schedule or deadlines
- Project budget
- The client's preferences

- Limitation and constraints
- Expected results

How to create a brief design

1) Start with a business overview.
2) Describe the key goals or objectives of the project.
3) Define the audience.
4) Understand the competition.
5) Set specific goals.
6) Set a schedule (timeline).
7) Set a budget.
8) Sum up everything.

Additionally, you can include the following:

9) A description of the results and the format in which they will be performed.

10) A description of the roles in the team that will be involved.

11) Restrictions or limits that exist in the product or project.

Ask the right questions. Projects are not built from solutions but from problems. Communicate well with projects that only give you an idea of a ready-made solution, but you need to know when the client thinks everyone will be his customers. To succeed, you need to have basic functionality. Brief only sometimes will be completed and structured; occasionally, you might receive notes, meeting minutes, or even a presentation deck requiring additional structuring and systematization.

Why do you need a design brief?

For business	For team
- Creates the basis for the relationship between the designer and the client. - Serves as a point of accountability for both the designer and the client. - Serves as a reminder of the design's purpose. - Creates trust between the client and the designer. - Is a sign of professionalism.	- Provides protection against unexpected changes in the scope of work. - Helps to plan.

Topic 3.6: UX Planning

A UX strategy is a detailed plan for aligning a company's identity with the desired user experience at every customer touch point. UX planning is a generic term that describes the definition of UX goals, plans, and activities that need to be performed to achieve those goals; it can be broadly divided into four stages:

1) **Business Strategy:** These are the company's guiding principles, as well as a competitive advantage, revenue streams, and high-level business goals.

2) **Value Innovation:** Companies achieve value innovation by seeking to gain value for customers (differentiation) while simultaneously reducing costs for the company.

3) **Proven user research:** Instead of guessing what is valuable to the customer, get direct input from your target users before starting development.

4) **Excellent user interface design:** Once the other principles are in place, it's time to create a user experience focusing on the product's key features.

There are also parallel processes that help us manage and plan the project from the UX point of view. They will include the following:

1) Stakeholder management.

2) Strategic planning of tasks and scope of work.

3) Prioritization of tasks and involvement of the team.

Topic 3.7: Stakeholders management

Stakeholder management is maintaining good relationships with the people who most influence your work.

1) Identify stakeholders, and make a general list with positions, and contacts, including the scope of responsibility.

2) Add them to the RACI or Stakeholder Matrix and give them the status of Defender, Supporter, Neutral, Critic, or Blocker.

3) Determine what you want from each stakeholder.

4) Write a communication plan.

Projects may change over time, so review your plan regularly. Typically this should be a collaborative document, so you could create it on your own or receive it from the team.

Why does it matter?

In many companies, those who work with you provide information and communicate decisions, and those who make decisions are different people. Stakeholder management allows you to divide them into categories according to the level of responsibility and involvement at the project's beginning. To ensure that your proposals and decisions are correct, you need to understand precisely who is the main person in their acceptance and agreement.

The first variant of stakeholder management is the **RACI matrix** (illustration 4). The acronym RACI stands for:

Responsible (R): The person who performs the task.

Accountable (A): The person who makes decisions and takes action on the task(s).

Consultant (C): A person to be consulted about the decision-making process and specific tasks.

Informed (I): the person who will receive information about decisions and actions during the project.

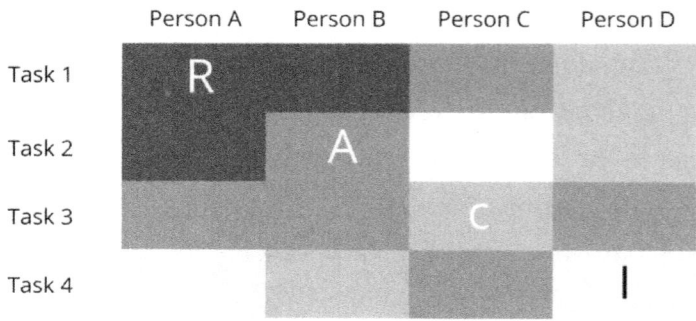

'Illustration 4: RACI matrix

Identifying "just" one person who is responsible or accountable is often challenging. If several people are reliable, dividing the activities is a good idea. The diagram defines four areas of responsibility; in practice, there are often more: you can determine external and internal stakeholders and include employees who participate at different stages.

As an alternative, a **stakeholder matrix can be used**. Stakeholder analysis identifies the most important stakeholders for a project, company, or product development with their interests, power, attitudes, and influence. A stakeholder matrix visualizes these stakeholders relative to each other on an XY graph. Some characteristics are presented as order characteristics and can be changed on the axes, for example, the influence of individual stakeholders — from low to high, the attitude to a specific project — from critical to positive, opinion — from fixed to open, power — from common to high, or interest — from low to high (illustration 5).

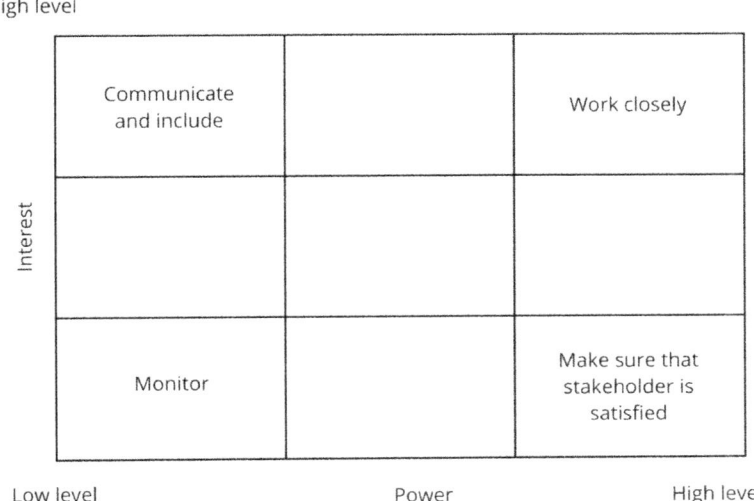

illustration 5: Stakeholder Matrix

A classic stakeholder matrix may contain, for example, influence and interest on the axes and stakeholder attitudes from damaging and neutral to positive.

An effective stakeholder management process will provide a means by which you can coordinate your interactions and assess the status and quality of your relationships with various stakeholders.

Topic 3.8: Scope planning

The next step we will consider in UX planning after management is scope and task planning. The purpose of scope planning is to ensure that all required work is clearly defined, that results are anticipated and planned, and that the project is completed successfully. Scope planning involves defining goals, objectives, resources, budget, and time frames. All results must be described in sufficient detail to distinguish them from inaccurate results. Scope management establishes control factors that can address issues that lead to change during the project life cycle.

Why should the scope be planned?

When we have a detailed enough scope - we know what we are building. This governance clearly describes what we are developing and how it relates to our goals. Scope planning helps with conflict management.

Scope documentation can be simple, but a common understanding of features, schedules, and milestones puts everyone on the same page and gives them a standard reference. It allows you to see the relationships between individual requirements that weren't clear and organize related conditions, which can help to determine which framework is suitable for your product.

Moreover, scope helps to narrow the field of possibilities and limit specific little creativity.

How is it done?

1) Collection of requirements: all or those related to specific functionality.
2) Prioritization and discussion of requirements.
3) Breaking them down into sprints, quarters, months (or whatever scheme works for you).
4) Expanding the requirements specification. Adding details and definition of done.
5) It breaks down complex individual tasks into smaller ones and distributes them among team members.

Definition of done (DoD) - a set of criteria that means that all the conditions or acceptance criteria a software product must satisfy have been met and are ready for approval by a user, customer, team, or consumer system. We must meet the definition of Done to ensure quality. This reduces rework by preventing user stories that do not meet the definition from moving to higher-level environments. This will prevent the delivery of features that do not match the report to the client or user.

In practice, scope planning is slightly different depending on the type of organization of your project. If we are talking about linear kinds of projects with a fixed budget, deadlines, and requirements, all documentation, including the scope of work, is created even before the start of the active phase of the project. Planning is carried out cyclically if the project is more flexible and is made according to the Agile or Lean methodology. The team is involved in defining, discussing, and communicating possible tasks. Discusses their potential duration and priorities for the study and how the results can be applied. All these data are recorded.

What happens if the scope is not planned or poorly planned?

- Deadline shift
- Too many questions
- Unrealistic expectations

The purpose of scope planning is to ensure that all required work is clearly defined, that results are anticipated and planned, and that the project is completed successfully. Scope planning takes place based on primary requirements from stakeholders, taking into account business and user needs, constraints, and vision.

Topic 3.9: Product Roadmap

A Product Roadmap is a shared source of truth that outlines a product's vision, direction, priorities, and progress over time. It is an action plan that aligns the organization around short-term and long-term goals for a product or project and how to achieve them.

Roadmaps can smooth alignment, improve strategic organization, and centralize team collaboration - no matter what project you're working on. An organization-wide road mapping process can help you put your business goals at the center so everyone can understand and act on them. This high-level document is a visual representation of the strategy: it answers questions about what will be done, who will be involved, details of scope and resource allocation, and how and why specific initiatives should be prioritized over others.

Ideally, a good roadmap should effectively communicate the following strategic elements:

- **Strategic Alignment:** Why (and how) initiatives align with higher-level business goals or product/business strategy.
- **Resources:** How the team will achieve these goals (e.g., OKRs) and what resources are needed.
- **Estimated time:** When any crucial deliverables are due.
- **Dependencies on other teams:** Which teams and team members to involve and why.

Why is a roadmap essential?

Like most attributes of strategic planning, a roadmap allows you to work with goals and resources. Roadmaps can create the transparent consensus needed to move forward with strategic decisions. They improve communication between teams and departments, creating an ongoing dialogue around strategy and goals. The visual aspect of roadmaps facilitates the transmission of results, schedules, projects, and initiatives within the organization.

How a Roadmap is created?

1) Assess where the company is today. How are your current efforts bringing you closer to achieving the company's vision and business goals?
2) Determine what you want to achieve. Research, SWOT analysis, and different goal-setting methods will help you.
3) Define success criteria. Do you have a way to measure success? How will you track progress?

4) When creating a roadmap, consider who your audience is. Add only as much detail as is necessary for her.

5) Keep the roadmap evenly focused on short-term tactics and how they relate to long-term goals. Review roadmaps regularly and make adjustments as plans change.

All roadmaps can be defined in one of 3 types:

- **Road map without dates.** Offers more flexibility than roadmaps built on timelines. It is helpful for companies whose priorities are constantly changing.

- **Timeline Roadmap.** Provides visual structure to the many moving parts that must work together to ensure business success. It also shows the long-term vision of the product, as some departments must plan for a year or more.

- **Flexible roadmap (Agile).** Illustrates how a product or technology will evolve with great flexibility. Unlike time-based roadmaps, which focus on dates and deadlines, flexible roadmaps concentrate on topics and progress. Many people think of any roadmap as a "statement of intent" because it means that plans can and will change.

Topic 3.10: Estimation

Estimating or assessing work duration is typical for any designer at the planning stage. It can be considered both from the point of view of time planning and from the point of view of resources, i.e., budgets. For example, a project cost estimate is a general idea of the project's pricing model. Estimating methods are methods of creating project estimates and timelines. When a client or other stakeholder asks you to evaluate an aspect of a project, these techniques will help you come up with a realistic figure that you can give them. With accurate estimates, it is possible to plan your project. In order not to guess but rather to estimate, there are many methods that you can apply.

The estimate can be:

- Actual (in days, hours, weeks)
- Relative (in story points)

Actual estimation determines that we can estimate the time required to complete the work based on experience, specific techniques, and information about the complexity.

In **relative,** we rely on evaluating the complexity of the work, which may not be directly proportional to the duration in time, so that the review will be determined in a certain proportional number of story points.

Three hours in the actual estimate can be equal to 1, 2, 3, or 5 story points. Evaluation in story points is usually performed in a team; you can use such tools as planning poker or t-shirt sizing.

Decomposition is separating into constituent parts or elements or simpler compounds. Decomposition involves breaking complex problems into smaller pieces that are easier to evaluate, compare, and investigate. Decomposition occurs where the task can be clearly described as a short step-by-step plan but not to the level where each point is a one-step task.

Analog method

It assumes that the one who will be the executor, or the one who estimates the duration, has performed a similar task before and knows how much time is required for this task. The system is built on the assumption that if a job took X hours last time, it will also take X hours this time.

It should be remembered that analog estimation is relative to a specific performer. The analog estimation will also depend on many factors, including the speed of the team, how much effort is spent on quality and complete performance of the task, availability of the necessary information before starting work, understanding of all details, and decomposition.

Three-point estimation

Three-point estimation is a technique used to estimate project duration. Instead of assuming one time for a task, you can assign three: optimistic (O), pessimistic (P), and realistic (R). These three numbers are averaged to create an actual score. The following formula is used to optimize and improve the estimation: the sum of the optimistic, pessimistic, and four realistic estimates is divided by 6.

$$(P + O + 4 * R)/6$$

There is another way to improve the score. This allowance for error protects us in unforeseen circumstances and provides a more accurate definition. The three-point estimate is entirely accurate, but it can be improved by using a double margin of error. The error in planning the task duration is a protective layer for the specialist, specific insurance in case of mistakes, revisions, unexpected changes, or even illness or vacation in the team.

The concept of error is two-sided. That is, from the calculated time, we can do the work faster by a step of error or longer by a degree of error. It is believed that twice the error added to the expected duration can guarantee a 90% accurate estimate. To determine the double error, we calculate the difference between the pessimistic and optimistic estimates and divide the value by 3.

$$(P + O + 4 * R)/6 + (P - 0)/3$$

Parametric estimation

For it, the number of involved people, technical complexity, the complexity of testing, and technologies used can be taken into account. In our case, for design estimation, we will consider estimating the complexity of the design task itself. In parametric analysis, the approach of level or coefficient of complexity is used. Each decomposed problem is evaluated and multiplied by the corresponding difficulty coefficient on a scale from 1 to 2, where:

1 is a straightforward task that was performed repeatedly,

2 is a challenging task that the team has not faced before.

And intermediate steps, for example, 1.2, 1.3. In this case, the difficulty is a more relative value, but the overall score will still be factual.

And if you need to evaluate tasks that have never been done before?

Decomposition will help you here. Small parts are easier to estimate, and the probability of the correctness of such an estimate is higher. Estimation of the task is ready for us to plan the work process for the teams - tasks and the customer - to build the right expectations. If we underestimate the task, it means unpaid overtime, an unhappy client, or going over budget when additional resources need to be brought in. If the estimate is significant, these are unrealistic indicators.

The estimate must be optimal and consider problems or changes, human factors, vacations, hospitals, etc.; we include these points in the margin of error. The slightest error that needs to be treated is about 2%, and the optimal one is about 7%.

You also need to choose the optimal step. If you estimate in days, note that although a typical working day is 8 hours, in practice, the time for busy work often remains about 5-6 hours, excluding meetings, calls, etc. This is individual for each organization, but you need to remember such a moment because it significantly affects the final assessment.

Topic 3.11: Prioritisation

Prioritization determines the level of importance and urgency of a task, thing, or event. Prioritization, like estimation, can be superficial or substantiated using different methods. Correct prioritization ensures the correct execution of tasks within the set deadlines.

How to do it:

1) Make a list of all your tasks.
2) Define urgent and essential.
3) Evaluate the value of your tasks scheduled for a certain period.
4) Communicate with the team or managers.
5) Organize tasks by estimated effort.

Tasks can be prioritized in project management programs, Excel, or even in a notebook if we talk about personal planning.

Eisenhower method

Prioritization, according to the Eisenhower method, helps to prioritize personal tasks and make plans. This approach may be appropriate if you need to prioritize tasks in a time management format. Former US President Dwight D. Eisenhower said, "I have two kinds of problems: urgent and important. Urgent is not important, and important is never urgent." The "Eisenhower

Principle" considers only two parameters: importance and urgency, avoiding complexity or duration of execution, which can also sometimes be very important.

- First of all, we always take on tasks that are important and urgent. If they are important but not urgent, this is the second priority; we can make a note of them or plan when exactly we will do them.
- Delegate unimportant but urgent tasks. Delegate them to another team member who can do it for you so that the work is still completed on time. You will do the essential things, and someone else will do the less important things. But you will still be responsible for both tasks.
- As for tasks that are not urgent and not important, delete them. Not literally. You can still leave them in the backlog, but you have other priorities until they become critical or essential.

This method is challenging for team prioritization, but it will work if we discuss micro-teams of 2-3 people.

Effort/Impact

The effort/impact matrix is sometimes called the action priority matrix, the effort/impact matrix, or the 2×2 matrix. It is often used to help establish project priorities at the outset.

The main principle of the matrix is a comparison of the effort spent on the task and the impact (on the business, on the user, and on the team that will perform the task). To use it, you need to draw a scale with coordinate lines "Influence" and "Effort" and place your tasks, goals, or functionality in the format of cards on this matrix (illustration 6).

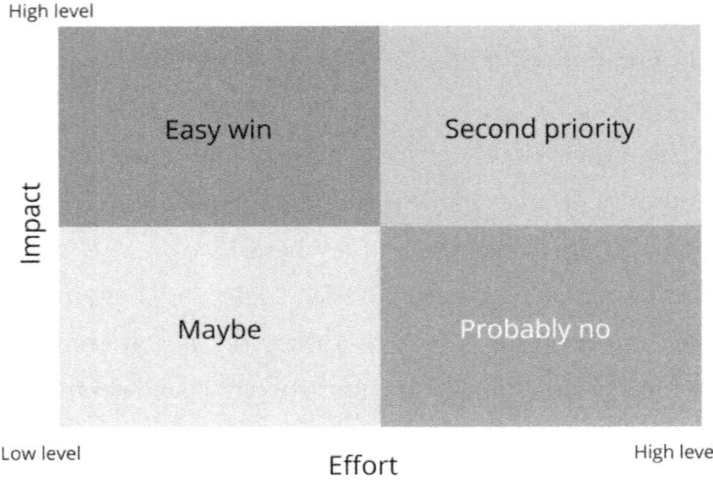

Illustration 6: Effort/Impact matrix

You can pick any other method you prefer, but it is essential to include various factors and parameters.

Topic 3.12: Design Sprint

A Design Sprint is a five-day process of answering critical business questions by designing, prototyping, and testing ideas with customers and users.

A sprint involves five stages and tasks that are solved within one working week:

- Understand
- Investigate
- Choose
- Create
- Test

Monday

Monday is a series of structured conversations to build the foundation and focus for the sprint week. In the morning, you will identify key issues and a long-term goal. Next, you'll create a simple map of your product or service. In the afternoon, you'll ask the experts on your team to share what they know. Finally, you will select a target: the highest risk and/or opportunity. Also, we need to schedule testing sessions for Friday.

Tuesday

Tuesday is all about problem-solving with a method optimized for deep thinking. There are creative activities of idea generation, probable search for solutions, analysis of competitors, and research.

A success criterion is formed to determine the best solution.

Wednesday

By Wednesday morning, you and your team will have a ton of decisions to make. Now you have to decide which one to prototype and test. Discussions, voting, prioritization, and refinement of the best options are carried out to facilitate the choice. Then, in the afternoon, the selected options are worked out by the team and analyzed in detail using the method of storytelling, creating a flow chart, or with the help of user stories.

Thursday

On Thursday, you will create a realistic prototype of the solutions in your storyboard (user flow, user story, sketching, etc.) to simulate the finished product for your customers. Design Sprint prototyping is a "fake it till you make it" philosophy.

Having a realistic prototype will give you the best data from Friday's test and know if you're on the right track.

Friday

It's time to test this prototype! On Friday, you will show your prototype to five users in five separate 1:1 interviews.

Instead of waiting for a launch to get perfect data, you'll immediately get quick and relatively unambiguous answers to the most pressing questions. The test results will be compiled into a document and presented to stakeholders.

How to conduct a design sprint

1) Determine the goal.
2) Gather a team of the right people.
3) Write a script.
4) Find a place and choose a time.

Preparation and proper facilitation are one of the main stages in conducting a sprint; you must be sure you understand how to work it, what activities you want to do, and how long each will take.

A design sprint is a fast way to generate and validate ideas based on design thinking. A properly planned sprint will allow you to go through a process in 1 week that usually takes several months.

Module 4: Defining the problem

Topic 4.1: Define

When starting work in the Double Diamond Discover phase, or Define in the Design Thinking framework, we define the problem. In a proper design process, we must define the problem, the circumstances, the environment in which the problem occurred, and the user or use case type. We can only move forward to research or generate ideas to solve this problem.

A problem statement is a concise description of the problem to be solved. This is a useful scoping tool that focuses the team on the problem they need to investigate and solve.

The statement of the problem explains what needs to be done during the research and what is beyond its scope. Problem formulation is also a great communication tool. Well-written statements can get stakeholders thinking about why it is essential to study and solve the problem.

How to formulate a problem statement

1) Consider the background of the problem. Which organization or department has a problem, and what is the problem? Why did the problem occur? In some cases, you may need to find out the exact cause of the problem, and the root cause will need to be discovered during the work process.

2) Who faced the problem? A particular issue may affect different groups of users differently. In your problem statement, you should state how the problem affects users.

3) Impact of the problem. If the problem is not solved, how will it affect the organization? Damage to reputation? Paying unavoidable expenses? Loss of market share? But how will it affect the user?

The 5W method can be used to describe the problem:

- Who - Who does the problem concern?
- What - What is the problem?
- Where - Where does this problem occur?
- When - When does the problem occur?
- Why - Why does the problem occur? Why is the problem significant?

A problem statement CAN NOT:

- Be a list of unrelated tasks. The Discovery phase should have one problem statement, and the problem statement should focus on one problem.
- Contain the solution. Leave the key out of the problem statement. At the beginning of the research, there were too many unknowns, so the best solution needed to be apparent.
- To be a whole brief. Problem statements are effective if they are concise. If you can reduce your problem statement to a few sentences, others will quickly understand what you are focusing on, why, and what is beyond the scope.
- The problem statement should not be harmful. It should indicate what we want to achieve.

Let's consider an example. A lousy problem: "Our customers complain about turnaround time, so we need to get faster." Let's paraphrase, add context and remove negativity: "We need to reduce design time by 50%, improve response time and communication, and complete tasks more thoroughly." In the second option, we define more clearly what we want to achieve and narrow the points we will influence.

Topic 4.2: To whom the problem relates too

In many cases, the correct wording ensures that the exact audience is defined. One of the first steps to problem-solving is understanding the target audience and the person's role. According to the number of the audience under consideration or the type of people included in it, the problems can be divided into:

- Problems of a specific person. Such cases are rare, large corporations will not pay attention to 1 person, especially if their audience is hundreds of times more significant, but there are exceptions.
- Group problems. A group, in this case, is a collective or a group of people with a unifying factor, such as a standard action they need to complete, a use case, a device they work with, or something else.
- People falling under a specific category or standard feature.
- Problems of a specific role. A role implies that it is not limited to a particular user; it can be individual or group, it is not limited by the environment or the type of device, and it is not determined by the characteristics of the person using it, his age, gender, physical parameters, etc.

Why can't the problem be solved "for everyone"?

If your problem has a broad audience and is faced by everyone, it is an ill-defined problem, or it has no solution. When we formulate a problem, we try to limit the spectrum of the audience that falls under it.

Defining the audience of the problem is essential for the completeness of its formulation and understanding of the case.

Problems need to be more familiar, their impact can be greater or lesser. There are also only so many universal solutions for all types of audiences.

Topic 4.3: Root cause

The root cause is defined as the factor that caused the discrepancy between expectation and reality and must be finally eliminated through process improvement.

A problem's root cause is the underlying problem—the top-level cause—that triggers the entire cause-and-effect reaction that ultimately leads to the problem. This is the main engine of the situation we must fix or improve.

To determine the root cause, you need to select the following:
- What is the problem?
- Why did this happen?
- What will be done to prevent this from happening again?
- How exactly does this affect?

Understanding the "Why did it happen" factor can cover the following:
- The primary motivation that explains why the events in which this problem was observed occurred.
- The cause or reasons for what happened and why we consider it a problem.
- Consequences, or how this problem affected the process or after its occurrence (is it possible to assess these consequences, were they the same for everyone, and the level of complexity of the products).

An example of describing the root cause of the problem:

"When users find an article they are interested in, they want to share it with friends and family. To do this, they often copy the text of the article and send it via messengers since not everyone knows how to send a link or share an article." Be aware that there may be many problems in a given situation, but you need to identify the root cause and focus on it, not the symptoms.

Topic 4.4: Problem's environment

To properly understand the problem, when we know who faced it and how we need to know the conditions that shape the environment. These "conditions" provide answers to the following questions:
- When?
- Where?
- What was happening at that moment?
- Is such a situation accidental or natural?
- Was there an additional influencing factor?
- Is there (was) another expected version of events?
- Why is this important?

Understanding the environment allows you to consider the situation more comprehensively to understand the real cause of the problem. It also allows us to clearly distinguish between different cases and target precisely the needed position.

Defining the environment will allow us to conduct additional research under the right conditions. When testing probable solutions, only testing in an environment as close as possible to the root cause will allow you to check the quality of the solution.

What we do NOT take into account:

- One-time, sudden circumstances that have NO logic and cannot be repeated.
- Circumstances in which the activity of the product is NOT foreseen.
- Individual circumstances that during the research were recognized as a single case (1 person or less than 0.1% of the number of respondents).

Example of environment description:

"Usually, readers read an online newspaper before or after the working day. Sometimes when commuting to work on public transport. Less often during the day in breaks. The average user usually reads 1-3 articles per day, which they navigate to from search or the hot news feed. When users find interesting articles or buzzy headlines that they want to share, they forward them to friends by copying the content."

This description of the environment gives us a broad understanding of the circumstances and situations in which a user might want to share an article from an online newspaper and under what conditions this might happen.

Topic 4.5: Fishbone diagram

A diagram is an artifact that allows us to depict and convey certain information visually without spending much time creating layouts. Charts are used by many specialists in the team and allow better communication.

I divide all diagrams on a typical project into technical and product types. I refer to technical diagrams related to system activity and its structure, for example, algorithm flowcharts, database diagrams, diagrams of interaction types, precedents, etc. Designers rarely interact with them.

Product diagrams are more related to user decision-making theory, such as various user flows, use case diagrams, and many others. Designers work more closely with them.

A fishbone diagram is a visualization tool for classifying potential causes of a problem. Other names you may come across are Ischicava diagrams, fish diagrams, cause and effect diagrams, or Fishicava diagrams. A fishbone diagram is helpful during product development and troubleshooting processes, typically used to focus the conversation around a problem. The diagram is used to validate the probable causes, categorize them and find the root cause.

When it is used:
- To determine possible causes of the problem.
- To help develop a product that addresses the challenges of current market offerings.
- To identify bottlenecks and weak points in the business process.
- To avoid repeated issues or employee burnout.
- To ensure that any corrective action taken will resolve the problem.

Fishbone diagrams are also helpful for future planning. By referring to the chart, teams can identify the best methods for achieving the desired results and plan actions accordingly.

When NOT to use a fishbone diagram:
- When one cause refers to several problems.
- When you are looking at correlation rather than causation.

Basic steps to create a fishbone diagram

1) The fish head is created by identifying the problem and drawing a frame around it. Then a horizontal arrow is marked on the page that points to the title. It acts as the backbone of a fish.

2) Then identify at least four leading "causes" that may contribute to the problem. Some general categories include methods, skills, equipment, people, materials, environments, or measurements.

3) Further, additional "reasons" are indicated on the "bones", expanding the "main ones" (illustration 7).

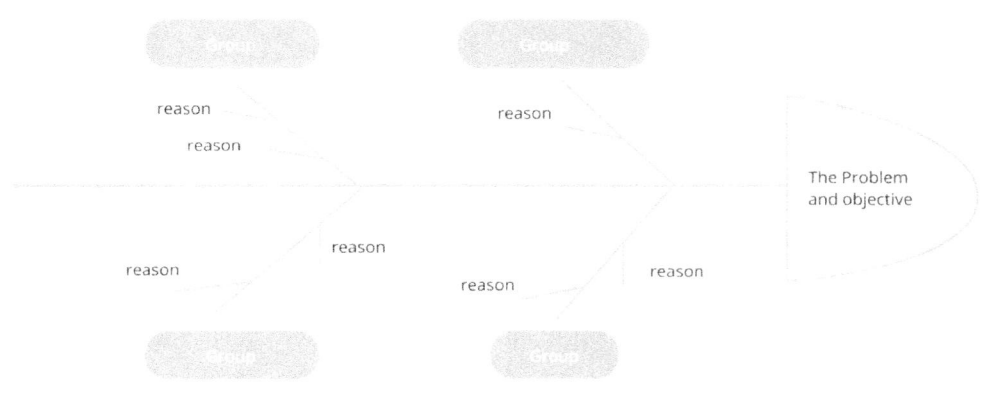

Illustration 7: Fishbone diagram

How to apply the results?

1) Develop a strategy based on how actions or inactions lead to positive or negative consequences.

2) More than analysis is needed if you want to change results and impact. Fishbone diagrams can help companies plan improvements to policies, management, systems, and more.

3) Analyze how conditions and motivations lead to actions and outcomes.

Topic 4.6: 5W method

A "5W" concept is an approach to problem analysis in the form of answers to questions considered essential for gathering information.

They include:

- Who?
- What?
- When?
- Where?
- Why?

And are combined into a formula to obtain a complete story and a comprehensive description of the situation. The approach is quite simple and overlaps with the general principles of forming a problem statement.

According to the 5W principle, a problem can be considered formulated only if it answers the following questions:

- What is it about?
- What happened?
- When did it happen?
- Where did it happen?
- Why did this happen?

Sometimes it is expanded with a question:

- How? Here "how" determines not how something happened but how we can deal with it, evaluate the solution to the problem, etc. Therefore, some call the use of an additional question the 5W and 1H method.

How to get answers to these questions? The key to getting a solution is always a question. You can ask people these questions, but be aware that it is difficult for people to give accurate answers simply by talking about what they do outside of the context of performing these tasks.

Instead, the best way to learn this information is to go out and observe (conduct a field study):

- Keep the people who will use your product.
- Watch what they are doing now and how they are doing it.
- Follow where they do it and when they do it.

This observation, combined with interviews, would answer why they do these tasks.

Why is it useful?

1) The answers to the questions allow us to outline a more comprehensive picture.
2) Understanding the different aspects can help clarify the root of the problem or help you realize that it is more profound than you thought.
3) The method helps to form an idea about the audience and the environment, which is especially useful when all users do not encounter the problem.

Topic 4.7: 5Whys

The "5Whys" method is a part of the Toyota Production System. This technology, developed by Sakichi Toyota, a Japanese inventor, and industrialist, has become an integral part of the Lean philosophy.

One of the critical factors in its successful implementation is making an informed decision. This means that the decision-making process must be based on a deep understanding of what is happening. In other words, people with practical experience should be involved in root cause analysis. It stands to reason that they can provide you with the most valuable information on any issue in their area of expertise.

Why does it work?

Using the "5 Whys" technique, you want to get to the bottom of the problem and fix it. The "5 reasons" may show you that the source of the problem is entirely unexpected. Often, what are considered technical problems that turn out to be human and process problems. Then the proposed changes will not concern the system's behaviour but the service part of the design.

How to conduct this activity?

1) Form a team. Try to assemble a team of people from different departments.
2) Identify the problem. Discuss the issue with the team and articulate it clearly. This will help you define the scope of the problem you will investigate.
3) Ask, "Why?" Help one person make the whole process easier. This team leader will ask questions and try to focus on everyone. Answers should be based on facts and accurate data, not emotional opinions.
4) The facilitator should ask "Why?" as often as necessary until the team can determine the root cause of the original problem.

So, the 5Why method is built on cyclical "Why?" questions to make a connection between the problem and the root cause. UX designers widely use it to research problems and find their root causes.

Topic 4.8: How might we

The "How Might We" method creates an environment for innovative solutions by rethinking known challenges surrounding your product, service, or initiative. Once you've identified design issues during expert interviews, you're ready to turn those statements into desirable questions that create a welcoming space for "outside" thinking.

The method is convenient for use in a team or independently. Writing How Might We Notes (or HMWs) is often practiced as a collaborative team exercise at the start of a project or strategic initiative.

How to do it

1) Start by identifying and outlining the thoughts or issues you've gathered about your current design challenge or new initiative.

2) Now rephrase these ideas into questions, starting each note with "How could we…."

3) When writing your question, consider the underlying factors that might be causing it—this is often the best way to clarify your initial thoughts.

4) Write as many "Would we" notes as possible.

5) If you use negative verbs like "reduce," "remove," and "prevent," ask yourself if you can frame the points more positively by using positive action verbs like "increase," "create," "improve," "promote," and so on.

6) Check your HMW for the following questions:

- Is this statement based on an existing problem or understanding?
- Is the desired result being tracked? Are you forcing your way to a solution?
- Is it written positively?
- Is the concept broad enough to provide many creative ideas?

There is no limit to the number of HMW questions you can create. The more you have, the more ideas you will get. If you find too many, ask yourself if there are any overlaps between them and see if you can combine some into one larger HMW. Another alternative is to prioritize your HMWs regarding their impact on project success.

The whole point of the method lies in formulating the right questions.

A well-phrased question: "How can we develop a product that makes our users confident and secure when doing financial transactions online?" In this case, we define what should happen and outline in what context.

An example of a very narrow and specific solution to the question: "How can we develop a product that helps users deposit salaries in three simple steps with a guided workflow?". In this case, it is not an open-ended sentence with room for creativity but rather a precise task with a predetermined expected result.

An example of a question that's too broad, "How can we build the world's most innovative banking app?" The space here is too open. We do not specify what innovation should be, classify who it should be designed for, or suggest a context. In this case, the opinions of our team will differ too much, and you will need help finding a standard solution.

Topic 4.9: Metrics and KPIs

No matter what product we develop, we need to consider the outcome. The result is not always a binary value of "success/failure"; it is a much larger understanding that includes various metrics and factors. The result can vary significantly on different projects.

KPIs

KPI, or Key Performance Indicator - measurable quantities used to assess how successfully a person or organization achieves a goal. You can have high-level KPIs that analyze your business performance or KPIs that detail individual or department-level processes.

How to work with KPIs

1) Write a clear goal for your KPI. It should be related to a critical business objective.
2) Share your KPIs with stakeholders.
3) Constantly review your KPIs. It is essential that you review your KPIs consistently. View your KPIs from two perspectives: your progress against the KPIs and your progress to determine KPI performance.
4) Create actionable KPIs. They are not static! Your key performance indicators (KPIs) should change as your business goals evolve. Analyze your current performance: are you setting achievable goals? Check your performance and the relevance of your KPIs.

Examples of business KRI	Examples of Product KPIs
- Net profit margin - 12% - Debt to equity ratio - 3.46 - The ratio of the total cost to the acquisition cost is 1.42	- Customer satisfaction according to SUS - >70 - Internal process quality - > 4 stars - Employee satisfaction - >80%

UX Metrics

UX indicators (metrics) - quantitative data used to monitor, measure, and compare interactions with a product over time. Unlike other metrics, such as sales, finance, or marketing, they are difficult to quantify because they reflect human behavior and attitudes.

Metrics are essential for measuring project progress, deliverables, and overall project success. Some areas where metric analysis is often required include resources, cost, time, scope, quality, safety, and operations.

UX metrics can be of different types:

- Descriptive metrics provide information about what happened and include usability metrics and accurate user monitoring.
- Perception metrics show how customers perceive what happened and are illustrated by engagement metrics.
- Outcome measures describe what customers did or are expected to do based on their perceptions. This category includes performance measures for adoption and user retention.

Examples of metrics

- Several user actions per session. It shows the user's actions and functions while working with the program.
- Net Promoter Score (NPS). This measure measures the proportion of loyal customers likely to recommend the product (promoters) and those who hate it (detractors). To calculate NPS, ask users to rate how likely they are to recommend your product (from 0 to 10). Detractors will rate this probability from 0 to 6 points, users with 7-8 points are neutral, and those who ordered the likelihood of recommending a 9 -10 are promoters. NPS formula: NPS = % promoters – % detractors.

- Traffic (paid/regular). The number of users who visited the site or a specific page and how it relates to the users' achievement of the overall goal.
- Bounce rate. This metric allows you to measure the percentage of users who visited just one page of a website or app and left.

The System usability scale is one of the metrics that can help us evaluate user satisfaction with our product.

The System Usability Scale (SUS) provides a "quick and dirty" but reliable tool for measuring usability. It consists of 10 questionnaire items with five answer options for respondents.

Here is an example of a typical question:

1) I want to use this system often.
2) The system needs to be simplified.
3) I found the system easy to use.
4) I will need support from a technical person to be able to use this system.
5) The various features in this system are well integrated.
6) There are too many contradictions in this system.
7) Most people will learn to use this system very quickly.
8) I found the system very cumbersome to use.
9) I felt very confident using the system.
10) I had much to know before starting to work with this system.

These questions are only indicative; you can adapt them to your needs and product features. As you can see, they are generally related to usability, but you can develop them for a specific feature or module of the product.

Success criteria

Success criteria, or Project success criteria - the standards by which the project will be evaluated at the end to decide whether it was successful in the

eyes of the stakeholders. They can be used for the entire project and individual modules or tasks.

Document your project's success criteria in list format. They can be added even at the stage of creating a design brief, but most often, the success criteria are projected to define the problem Define.

Each success criterion should contain:
- The name of the success criterion.
- How will it be measured.
- How often will it be measured.
- Who is responsible for its measurement.

There are typically two options for measuring project success criteria:
- Discrete (binary): "yes/no" (we did or did not do something), for example, the project was completed on time, the company received X accreditation, a new branch was opened.
- Continuous: Measurable on a scale (we've done something to some degree, within the target range), such as increasing customer satisfaction to 75-100%, increasing revenue by 8-10%, rebranding 15-20 offices during the fourth quarter, etc.

Success criteria are determined individually for each task or activity. They can be divided into two types:

1) Criteria that are related to project management. For example: hold a meeting of the project board once a month, and complete the project audit according to the schedule.

2) Criteria that are related to project results. For example, get the software rolled out to all users and train 95% of staff within a two-week training period.

Working with metrics, KPIs, and success criteria is essential at many stages. You need to clearly understand why you are setting this indicator, what it will affect, and in what timeframe, and have an idea of how it can be achieved.

Module 5: UX research

Topic 5.1: Types of user research

User research focuses on understanding user behaviors, needs, and motivations through interviews, surveys, usability evaluations, and other feedback methodologies.

When starting the conversation about research, they are of different types and complexities and can be adapted to the needs and available resources. One of the first steps in developing a new product or improving the experience of an existing product is to start thinking about your users:

- Who are they?
- Where are they from?
- What do they want?
- Why do they want this?
- How can your product help them get what they want?

As a UX researcher, you have to answer these questions. Instead of making best guesses based on your subjective experience, you'll develop a research strategy to answer these questions based on data.

Although UX researchers have borrowed methods from academic, scientific research (especially psychology), many forms of UX research are unique to the field. The primary goal of UX research is to articulate user needs using a user-centered approach.

There are such types of research:

Quantitative	Qualitative
Behavioral	Attitudinal

Behavioral answers to the question of what people do, and attitude answers to the question of what people think. Qualitative tells you why they do it and how it can be fixed, while quantitative tells you how many people do it, how much they like or dislike it, etc. (illustration 8).

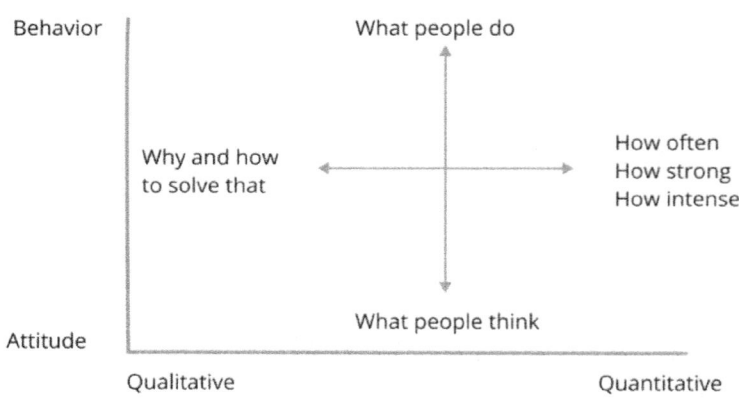

Illustration 8: Types of user research

Why is user experience research important?

In the first place, to reduce uncertainty at each decision-making stage. By understanding users, their wants, and needs, we can inform the UX design process to create the optimal product for users, creating business benefits.

84

Product Benefits: UX research is essential to shaping design strategy and decisions made at every stage of the design process. The data collected in UX research helps prioritize ideas and features, formulate user stories, and make informed decisions about how the product will work and look. This upfront investment in research and continuous testing will ultimately optimize the development process and create a product that does exactly what it needs to do – no more, no less.

User benefits: Taking the time to understand users leads to products, programs, services, or improvements that are useful, desirable, accessible, trustworthy, easy to find, practical, and valuable.

Business Benefits: UX research is one of the most essential parts of building an app or website, directly impacting customer acquisition, conversion, retention, lifetime value, loyalty, and generating referrals. If you know who your users are and what they want, you'll likely create a product that's somehow undervalued - and it'll be hard to understand because of a lack of research. UX research, on the other hand, can inform what needs to be built and the ROI achieved. Reasonable solutions can also save money by reducing development time and eliminating costly redesigns.

Quantitative research

Quantitative research deals with numbers and graphs. The method is used to test or confirm theories and assumptions. This type of research can be used to establish general facts about a topic.

Standard quantitative methods include experiments, observations recorded as numbers, and surveys with closed questions.

Data collection methods:

- Survey: A list of closed-ended or multiple-choice questions administered to a sample (online, in person, or by telephone).
- Experiments: Modeling a situation where variables are controlled and manipulated to establish cause-and-effect relationships.
- Observation: Observing subjects in a natural environment where variables cannot be controlled.

Qualitative research

Qualitative research deals with words (emotions, thoughts, etc.). The method is used to understand concepts, thoughts, or experiences. This type of research provides insight into topics that need to be better understood.

Standard qualitative methods include open-ended interviews, narrative observations, and literature reviews that explore concepts and theories.

Data collection methods:

- Interview: oral questioning of open-ended questions to respondents.
- Focus groups: A discussion of a particular topic among a group of people to gather opinions that can be used for further research.
- Ethnography: Participating in a community or organization to observe culture and behavior closely over an extended period.
- Literature review: a review of published works by other authors.

The difference between quantitative and qualitative research

Some UX activities might be used for qualitative and quantitative research, and their outcome will be connected to the goals and metrics used to assess the activity's success.

Quantitative research	Qualitative research
- Focuses on testing theories and hypotheses.	- Focuses on exploring ideas and formulating a theory or hypothesis.
- It is analyzed using mathematical and statistical analysis.	- It is analyzed by summarizing, classifying and interpreting.
- It is mainly expressed in numbers, graphs and tables.	- Mostly expressed in words.
- A large number of respondents is required.	- A small number of respondents is required.
- Closed questions (with one or multiple answer-options).	- Open questions.
- Key terms: testing, measurement, objectivity, reproducibility.	- Key terms: understanding, context, complexity, subjectivity.

To conduct any research, you need to go through the following five steps:

Determine what you need to know about your users and their needs to make a decision.

1) Ask yourself: What do you think you already know about your users? Each hypothesis is a testable assumption about user behavior and potential solutions to meet user needs.

2) Next, consider which research methods to use based on your deadline, project type, and the size of your research team.

3) Using your chosen research method(s), start gathering data about your users, their goals, and their needs.

4) Analyze the collected data to fill in the gaps in your knowledge, proving or disproving each hypothesis, and create a plan to improve your product based on user feedback.

- Use quantitative research when you want to confirm or test something (a theory or hypothesis).
- Use qualitative research if you want to understand something (concepts, opinions, experiences).

5) As you select and prepare to conduct research, remember the four principles of good research:

- Show empathy. Try to get to know your users, their mindset, and their needs. Try to reduce the bias of what you think you know and focus only on the user without any specific goal or outcome.
- Be open. Avoid making preconceived assumptions about the user, the problem, the solution you want to create, or what most users do or think. Instead, consider that a minority of users may have opportunities to offer important information about new products or features. Be prepared to be proven wrong at the research stage.
- Research everything. While any research is better than no research, the most significant value comes from researching at every stage of UX design to ensure you're designing the right product – and the product is designed right.
- Small tests can also be helpful. Not every research method needs quantitative data. Keep in mind that many quality methods provide sufficient feedback on features and improvements with only a small number of users.

When choosing a research method, pay attention to the goal and purpose. However, any research is better than guesswork, even based on personal experience.

Topic 5.2: User Persona

When it comes to the audience and methods of working with it, such methods as creating a persona or proto-persona come to the fore. These precious UX tools allow you to understand your target audience better and make design decisions accordingly. They are based on the concept of personification, or prototyping of a potential user. We want not only to have a general idea of who our potential audience is but also to have a list of specific features that will help us clearly define it and narrow down the circle.

Persona

The concept of impersonification is closely related to the development of empathy. When creating a product, we assume the role of our users and look at a situation or problem from their point of view.

User personas are descriptions of typical users whose goals and characteristics correspond to the needs of a larger group of users.

Usually, a persona is presented as a one- or two-page document. Such 1-2 page descriptions include:

- Behavior patterns
- Purposes
- Skills
- Attitude
- Background information
- As well as the environment in which the person works.

Avoid additional details that cannot affect the design.

Why might using a persona be important?

1) It develops empathy. The persona guides us in making decisions.

2) A persona adds personalization and helps us remember why and for whom we are creating a product, which helps avoid "design for design's sake."

How to create a persona?

1. Collect information about your users.

2. Identify patterns of behavior from research data.

3. Create a persona and prioritize.

Signs of a quality persona:

- Personas are NOT made-up assumptions about what the target user thinks. Each aspect of the personality description must be linked to actual data (observations and research).

- Personas reflect actual user patterns, not different user roles. Personas are NOT a reflection of roles in the system.

- A persona focuses on the current state (how users interact with the product) rather than the future (how users will interact with the product).

- A persona is context specific (it focuses on behaviors and goals related to a particular product area).

The persona includes:

1) The person's name (a simple fictional name or, if there will be many people, you can add numbers, for example, Shawn First, Mark Second, etc.).

2) Photo (can be a stock image or you can use a random face generator on the Internet).

3) Demographic data (gender, age, location, marital status, family).

4) Goals and needs (what a person wants, needs, and why).

5) Frustrations (or "pain points").

6) Behavior description (focus on situations or environments relevant to your case).

7) Identity details (such as a quote or tagline that conveys identity).

Having created a persona, present it to the team, and tell in detail why you chose such a persona, its characteristics, features, and clarity of vision.

There can be several personas. This usually happens when we portray personas of different roles. Even though the persona is not the personification of the role itself, combining them into one persona is challenging, or if the difference between other groups of users is too significant to generalize them into one.

Proto-persona

If a persona is not based on research but only on assumptions, it is a proto-persona - a prototype that will require verification and validation.

A proto-persona describes a product's target users and audience based on stakeholder assumptions.

Creating this custom persona allows product teams to start designing and building immediately without getting bogged down in the details of user behavior. Because these personas are developed using the prior knowledge and assumptions of stakeholders and team members, they need to be updated with any new information or analysis gained during the project.

Advantages of using a proto-persona:

- Creates a shared vision for the entire team.

- Helps you prioritize and focus.

- Iterative.
- Allows you to basically draw out the audience and describe the user (which can be helpful when finding respondents for interviews or surveys).

How to create a proto-persona

1) Create a proto-persona as a team.
2) Start with the prospect's name and basic information.
3) Add points that will be important when selecting users, for example, approximate age or profession. However, don't go into too much detail, it will limit you, but it will still only be a guess.
4) Use a template with stickers or an interactive whiteboard online so that the proto-persona can be viewed or added to by all team members.
5) Discuss ready-made proto-personas.

The easiest way to visualize a proto-persona is a 2x2 matrix (illustration 9).

In the first quadrant, add a photo or image of the potential user, and add a name or a nickname. Briefly describe her demographic characteristics, age, profession, and features in the following. Then focus on behaviors and values, as well as goals and needs. Think about what motivates you and what might be a problem for your proto-persona.

When choosing a proto-persona or persona, be guided by your goals and available input. In general, you can do both, starting with a proto-persona as an assumption and moving toward a persona based on research and validation of your premises.

	Behaviour and values
Who is that? Name or Nickname	What do they like? What is important for them?
Demographical data Occupation Age Gender Marital status	**Goals and needs** What are they trying to achieve? What bothers them? What goals do they have?

Illustration 9: Proto-persona matrix

Topic 5.3: JTBD or what if Persona doesn't work

Jobs-be-done (JTBD) is a framework based on the idea that when users "hire" (i.e., use) a product, they do so for a specific "job" (i.e., to achieve a specific result). A set of "tasks" for a product is an exhaustive list of user needs.

Quite often, JTBD completely replaces the concept of a persona. The framework represents user needs from qualitative user research such as field studies, interviews, and usability testing.

Compared to user personas, JTBD is a relatively new framework. It builds on traditional methods such as tasks. It uses case analysis but turns it on its head, moving away from what is "the user's task or how to accomplish it" and shifting

93

the focus to what outcomes the user wants to achieve and what functions it needs for this.

According to JTBD, there are three types of needs; let's consider them using the example of buying headphones.

1) **Functional needs:** The ability to listen to music, podcasts, etc., and talk during calls in comfort, long battery life, fit into the budget, and only take up a little space in the luggage.

2) **Social needs (or emotional):** Creates a user view of premium products (stylish design, brand, or popular model), not hearing voices/sounds around you.

3) **Personal needs:** Comfortable fit in or on the ears, easy to maintain, clean, or repair.

The advantages of JTBD:

- It reduces bias by moving away from who users are, where they live, what they do, and toward what they want to do.
- JTBD is helpful to use at the very beginning of the process when decisions are made that define the overall direction and purpose of the program.
- The method ensures that users achieve their goals with your product.
- It can help generate more inclusive solutions by not making only assumptions about what users want.

But JTBD also has disadvantages:

- In general, the method is built on removing humanizing elements. Thus the attitude to such a description is more technical than empathetic.
- The technique is still susceptible to conjecture.

- JTBD is not a method for identifying pain points, so it will not help work with an existing project if the goal is to place less successful features and interactions that need to be improved.

Models of the formation of story jobs, which is the primary way of presentation in JTBD:

A simple model	
Action + Object + Context	Action - Improve. Object - Podcast listening experience. Context – Minimizing external sound.
An optimal model	
Situation + Motivation + Result	Situation – When I listen to podcasts. Motivation – I want to not be distracted by external sounds. Result - So that I can be more focused on the information.

Generated JTBDs require validation. To do this, you can conduct user surveys and prioritization.

A simple way to rate is a Likert scale (from 0 to 10). We will ask customers how vital "the job" is and how satisfied they are with their product. Next, we can place the obtained results on a coordinate line and compare their Importance and Satisfaction with them.

When prescribing the item "result" according to JTBD, it is essential to consider different types:

- The desired results that clients want to achieve.

- Undesirable outcomes that clients seek to avoid.
- The desired results that the business wants to achieve.
- Undesirable outcomes that the business seeks to avoid.

Working with these "results" can also help with prioritization.

JTBD can be applied to work with existing products to improve them and address new opportunities. This method allows you to build connections between specific and probable new solutions. Therefore, it is well-used for products that involve digital transformation.

When JTBD is applied to innovation, a map of new and existing solutions can additionally be applied. This will help you build connections and draw parallels with your competitors.

For example:

Story: I want to listen to music on my phone without paying for each track.

The existing solution is Apple Music, and the new one is Spotify. In other words, a shift from purchasing music to subscription music.

Story: I want clean and healthy teeth to look good and visit the dentist less often.

The existing solution is an ordinary toothbrush; the new solution can be an electric or automatic toothbrush, and other types that will be better or at least different in the method of solving the problem, but the same in the work that needs to be done.

Topic 5.4: User Interviews

An interview is one of the most popular and practical activities in UX design. They allow you to collect data from the first person and discuss various hypotheses. Interviews are often the primary source of information for a future product.

A user interview is a UX research method in which a researcher asks a single user question about a specific topic (such as system usage, behavior, and habits) to learn more.

Unlike focus groups, which involve multiple users simultaneously, user interviews are one-on-one sessions (although sometimes multiple facilitators may take turns asking questions).

Several options for interview goals:

- Gather information and develop empathy even before starting to create a design or form a possible solution.
- Validate assumptions.
- Learn more about user habits, needs, and pain points.
- Analyze user behavior with an existing product or a new prototype.

Interviews can be of different types:

Structured interviews are precisely the same for each participant and are designed to gather information from different users. The questions are mostly "closed", and do not allow many explanations. Sometimes the questions will require answers in the form of multiple choice or scales.

Semi-structured interviews have some structure but leave plenty of room for discussion. The researcher creates a discussion plan or test scenario that helps guide the conversation in a direction that provides valuable information for the design team. This will usually include scenarios or tasks to push the participant forward.

When conducting an **unstructured interview**, there is no plan or script but rather some very open-ended questions. This allows the user to control the conversation.

Conduct user interviews if your question or problem needs further investigation or if you need to understand how others feel about your topic. Also, if you want to ask back and react to what your respondents have to share.

Interviews work great in the early stages of developing a concept or product. Also, it can provide insight when researching existing solutions when you ask people for their opinions on a product and their experience using it.

Advantages of the interview

- Quality of conclusions
- Time for changes and reaction
- Comprehensive feedback
- Revealing hidden possibilities

Disadvantages of interviews

- Involved resources (time, people, money).
- The quality of each interview does not imply the overall quality.
- Summarizing the discussion is often the most challenging part of the task.

Processing the interview results, especially qualitatively, requires skills and considerable time.

UX Design Essential Handbook: Beginner to Junior UX designer

Topic 5.5: Preparing for User Interview

Techniques of planning and organizing interviews can be applied to any other such activities, for example, subject interviews with experts in your project field.

Conducting an interview is a formulaic and iterative process in planning. Let's divide it into three stages: **preparation, conducting,** and the **period after the interview.**

Before the interview or Preparation

1) Define the goals.
   - What exactly do you want to know?
   - What results will be helpful to you?
2) Choose an interview format.
3) Make a list of questions, an interview outline, or a detailed script.
4) Screen potential participants.
5) Reserve a place and time and invite participants.

During the interview

1) Start a conversation, offer the participant tea or coffee, have small talk, and go with short questions that will help you start a conversation.
2) Begin the interview with an intro. Describe the purpose and plan, and explain exactly what will happen and why this session is being held.
3) Enable audio/video recording (remember to get permission).
4) Ask questions according to the created plan, and follow the timeline.

After the interview

1) End with a thank. At the end of the verbal part of the interview, ask the user to fill out a questionnaire or an additional feedback form.
2) Take the participant's contacts for future sessions.

Period after interview

1) Digitize the records and analyze the results.
2) Prepare a report.

Screening process

To recruit research participants, you should ask probing questions that assess their background and characteristics.

Purpose of screening:

- Obtain specific information about users and ensure that participants are existing or potential users of the desired product.
- Avoid revealing particular details on the study.

Screening can be carried out independently by designers or analysts or delegated to special recruiting agencies or departments in the company. In both cases, you must prepare a list of questions with expected answers to determine whether a particular person can become a member.

For screening, use open-ended questions that invite people to answer in their own words rather than choosing from a list of predetermined answers. Since there are no answer options, it is difficult for people to guess which answer is "correct."

Questions can be different, generalized, or more specific. Example,

1. Demographic indicators: age, gender, ethnicity, location, marital status.

2. Work experience: position, company size, employment status, and industry.

3. Level of experience with specific software and tools.

4. Frequency of use.

5. Technical savvy.

Pay attention to the fact that the screening should not lead people to understand the interview topic and be quite open.

Some tips for selecting participants:

- Think about how much information you need: the more complex the situation you're investigating, and the less you know about it, the more people you'll need to talk to. Depending on the complexity, you can plan to recruit from 6 to 10 participants.

- Break down important subgroups in your pool of potential interviewees (for example, if you need to talk to representatives of several age groups). In this case, you can get 3-5 people from each subgroup, so multiply accordingly.

- Add two or three additional interviews to your practice list if you have not yet conducted open-ended interviews before or none at all. If all goes well, you'll even have additional data.

Four rules of a comfortable interview

1) Maintain eye contact.
2) Allow the participant to speak, do not interrupt.
3) Be polite, friendly, and interested.
4) Use situational questions that help the user imagine rather than recall.

And the bonus: it is better to let a satisfied user go without the necessary information than to spoil the experience.

Based on the interview results, you will need to prepare a report. In the context of UX research, the report you share outside your research team is likely closer to an executive summary: a short, high-level document emphasizing the following steps and business application than methodology.

The interview report should be:

- A summary of the data and results of the study.
- Well written with a standardized structure.
- Informative, often with links, charts, images, and other data sources.
- The basis for decision-making.

You can find many examples of interview plans and reports on the Internet; they can be a good base. However, remember that in any case, the preparation for each series of interviews should be thoughtful and thorough.

Topic 5.6: Writing interview script

Interviewing users is a great way to gain insight into their experiences, needs, and wants. With this in mind, formulating questions requires some thought and attention.

We can use different types of questions:

- **Open-ended** questions are questions that can be freely answered. They usually give room for discussion and do not limit the user. For example, "How satisfied or dissatisfied are you with this process? What would you expect if you did...(a certain action)?" The point of open-ended questions is to get more complex answers than yes/no; they allow you to develop and maintain a conversation.
- **Closed-ended** questions can be answered with "yes" or "no" or have a limited set of possible answers (e.g., A, B, C). An example of a closed question can be: "Are you satisfied? Did it work as you expected?" It would be best if you were more careful with closed questions, they do not always

give the necessary level of detail, but they can make the conversation more formal and strict.

- **Leading questions** prompt the user by inadvertently suggesting an answer. Why do you like using X so much? Such questions are not entirely fair because they impose a specific answer format on the user.

Examples of questions by topic:

1) Questions for getting to know each other
   - Tell us about your role at work.
   - What did you do last weekend?

2) Questions aimed at detailing
   - When was the last time you did [activity]?
   - Tell me about how you are currently solving [problem]?
   - Have you used any other tools before to solve [problem]?

3) The question of the conformity of the product to the market
   - What is your team's current budget for [activity]?
   - Please describe your experience with [tool].
   - If you were looking for [information], where would you expect to find it?

4) General question
   - Tell me about how you and/or your team use our product.
   - What do you wish our product could do that it can't do today?

You decide what your script will look like. When broken down into simple steps, you need an intro and opening statement, a middle part with questions, and a wrap-up, which you will distribute in a 45-90 minute session.

Here is a typical script outline:

- Intro - 3-5 minutes.
- Introductory information - 2-3 minutes.
- Permissions and approvals - 2 minutes.
- Icebreaker or warm-up - 10-15 minutes.

- Basic questions - 30-45 minutes.
- Additional questions - 5-15 minutes.
- Summary - 3 minutes.
- Completion - 2 minutes.

About 90 minutes together.

Sample of the script for a typical interview:

Intro	*"Hello, my name is [moderator]. Today I will conduct our interview. As I mentioned in the email, we are currently developing a product with [Product] for [broad purpose].* *I would like to start by thanking you for taking the time to speak with us. Your feedback is valuable and will be used to inform our team about future design decisions. Duration of this interview [duration; for example, 60 minutes]. Is it right for you? If you need a break or stop at any time, please let me know. During this interview, I will ask you some questions about [topic]. Keep in mind that there are no wrong answers - you are the expert here! We conduct interviews like this to hear things from your perspective."*
Permission to record	*"It is important for us to keep detailed answers, how do you feel about the audio/video recording of our session? These materials are for internal use only and will not be shared with third parties."*
Warming up	*"To begin with, I would like to hear a little about you. What is your profession? Is it something that requires special training or experience? What goals do you set for yourself in your work? What motivates you?"*
Let's move to the topic	*"Thank you for this context. Now I would like to ask you a few questions about [topic].* - *If you had to explain it in the simplest terms, how would you do it?* - *How does [topic] relate to your goals in doing your job?* - *What do you do when you have questions about [topic]?* - *What would you like to see clearer about [topic]?"* *[Follow by more project specific questions]*

| Conclusion and summaries | *"Thank you very much for your time. Your opinion is very important to us, and it will significantly affect the improvement of the quality of our product."* |

The list of questions ensures that you:

- Will have the opportunity to get feedback from your team on your pre-interview questions.
- Learn everything you want to know and ask users about as many similar topics as possible during interviews.
- Ask clear, non-leading questions.
- Overcome stress or fatigue by having questions at hand to refer to.

Test it with your friends and colleagues if you work with a moderated and structured script. Make sure the questions are clear, open-ended, and connected to make the process easier for the user. This process is called a dry run.

When formulating a question, remember that the conversation should not be like an interrogation but rather positive, and include a two-way conversation, when you, for your part, will not only read the questions and note down the answers but also ask clarifying questions, maintain the conversation and you will be maximally included in the process.

Topic 5.7: Affinity mapping

Affinity mapping is a tool that organizes elements into groups of similar elements - instrumental when analyzing qualitative data or observations.

Typically, user research is considered through thematic analysis. In thematic analysis, you seek to make sense of all the notes, observations, and discoveries you have documented across all your sources of information, creating themes to organize the information and build through lines for each idea.

Using this approach, we want to understand the following:

- User moods and facial expressions (behavior) when performing specific tasks.
- Frequently used words or phrases when describing a product or user experience.
- Suggestions for improving your product or user experience.

How to create such a diagram?

1) Data from a series of interviews or other research or observations should be recorded on individual cards, stickers, or labels.
2) Look for related patterns in notes or observations and group them.
3) Create a group for each pattern or theme and give each theme or group a name.
4) Summarize what you learned about each group (give your analysis or critical idea).
5) This activity is not just for analysis; it is an effective cross-stage tool that can be used when:
   - Your brainstorming is over, and you need to sort and thematize your ideas or proposals.
   - You are solving a complex problem, and there are too many thoughts.
   - You have conducted research, interviews, idea generation, or other activity, and there are too many ideas or data.
   - You tend to think outside the box and believe there are deeper patterns in your information than those that catch the eye at first glance.

When creating an affinity diagram, invite people of different specializations. Of course, this can also be done individually, but it can be easier with a group.

Topic 5.8: Empathy mapping

Another way to analyze the results of interviews or other studies is to form an empathy map.

An empathy map is a collaborative visualization to articulate what we know about a specific type of user.

It externalizes knowledge about users to:

1) Create a shared understanding of user needs.

2) Help in decision-making.

In HCD (human-centered design), empathy maps are best used early in the design process. Keep the empathy maps "live" by reviewing and adjusting them as you explore further.

Empathy cards are used because:

- They help us understand the needs and goals of our users in a more nuanced but organized way.
- Empathy maps can be read and understood quite quickly.
- They may be used to collect data directly from users.

Creating an empathy map is easy, but this activity takes time.

How to create such a diagram?

1) Define scope and objectives.
   - What user or persona are you visualizing?
   - Why are you making a map?

2) Prepare the materials. A large board, stickers, markers for the team, or an online board.

3) Gather the research you will use for your empathy map. You will need qualitative inputs: interviews, field studies, diary studies, listening sessions, or qualitative surveys.

4) Read the study individually, fill in the stickers, display them in the four quadrants, and add notes to the map on the board.

5) Group similar notes that belong in the same quadrant, and name the clusters with topics representing each group.

The Empathy Map consists of 4 quadrants (illustration 10), each of which includes a summary or specific observation that relates to the user: what the user Says, Does, Feels, and Thinks about the product, project, particular problem, or in general in regards some topic.

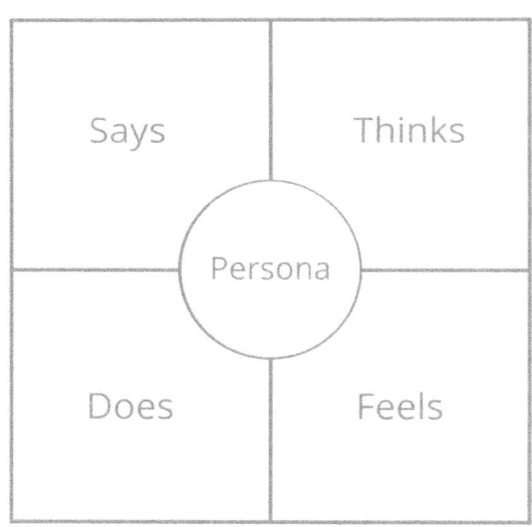

Illustration 10: Empathy map

The **Says** quadrant contains what the user says out loud during an interview or other usability study. Ideally, it should contain verbatim and direct quotes from research.

The **Does** quadrant captures the actions the user takes. We want to know what the user is physically doing based on the research results. How is the user going to do this?

The **Thinks** quadrant captures what the user is thinking throughout the experience. Try to understand why they are reluctant to share - are they insecure, polite, or afraid to tell others?

The **Feels** quadrant is the user's emotional state, often represented as an adjective plus a short sentence for context. Ask yourself: what is bothering the user?

It must be understood that the empathy map and mapping is only a UX tool, not a solution to change organizational thinking. The purpose of the exercise is to put the user in the center of the participants' thoughts.

Based on empathy mapping, you can also conduct workshops to unite the team in understanding the project and the problems you are solving and help team members better understand the user.

Topic 5.9: UX survey

A UX survey is a quantitative study in the form of a set of questions sent to a target group of users, testing their attitudes and preferences. Surveys can be a quick, easy, and inexpensive way to get the data you're interested in. A poorly designed survey will not provide valuable information.

Surveys are a popular solution due low cost of creation and high level of involvement, but also, it's less personal. It might be quickly impacted by several users who answer incorrectly or not entirely.

Six rules for creating a questionnaire

1) Try to ask a neutral question. Always try to ask something neutral, and avoid leading questions, as this will not add any value to your research.
2) Include easy questions. Stick to explicit language, meaning, and context for all questions. If you need clarification from Google, you have not done your job effectively.
3) Respect your user's anonymity. Privacy means everything to users! Make sure users feel confident providing information to you.
4) Ask one concept at a time. Avoid questions that contain two different concepts. This isn't very clear and also degrades the quality of your data.
5) Use the balance of the rating scale. If you put more positive options first, people are likely to choose one favorable option even if they want to say something terrible to you, so differentiate the responses.
6) Give real choices or alternatives. When asking questions, always remember that the options you provide may not apply to some users. They may perceive and do it differently.

To create a survey questionnaire:

1) Understand the purpose.
2) Prepare the Questionnaire.
3) Test it. Do a dry run with your team or friends.
4) Add screening.

5) Publish or send.

Questions in UX surveys can be divided into the following categories.

Questions about user expectations and impressions. This UX research question is closely related to user expectations and experiences. We want to know the feelings (related to customer satisfaction) of respondents who interact with our features, website, product, or service. This research stage also allows us to check user expectations compared to our proposed solution.

General questions for feedback. This group of questions aims to gather feedback about the respondent's contact with the website, product, or service. We ask respondents to complete a specific task and then examine the effort expended to do so.

Questions about the usability of a specific task. This group of UX design research questions works very well when testing websites, SaaS products, or new features we want to test before launching on the market.

General feedback questions check the impression of the whole process. Used to understand the general feel of the user about the product and details related to specific functionality.

Questions (tasks) about the usability of specific tasks involve an in-depth analysis of each stage.

Examples of questions

- Tell us about your experience with {product or app name}?
- How would you rate the usability of {product or app name}'s interface?
- Given that you've used our interface extensively, are you likely to recommend it to your friends and colleagues?

- How would you describe {app or product name} in one or more words?
- If [app or product name} were a car, what car would it be?
- How does {app or product name} compare to {competitor}?
- If you were to leave a review for {app or product name}, what rating would you give out of 10? And other.

The questions we apply must be correctly formulated.

Good questions	Bad questions
Task-oriented feedback questions. For example, "Tell me about your experience using your current banking application."	The question is "yes or no". These are closed questions, meaning you can't really get more information.
Open-ended questions about expectations or impressions. For example, "What is your favorite feature?"	Assumption. In particular, we mean questions that involve positive or negative experiences, such as: "What did you dislike most about this feature?"
Clarifying questions. For example, "How would you rate your experience using the app?"	Suggestive questions. This is bias. For example, "If you like this product, should we make more like it?"

Topic 5.10: Diary study

A Diary study is a contextual, qualitative research methodology used to record users' behavior, activities, and experiences.

It is more than just a "human study." Once you start working, you'll notice that the methodology offers some unique advantages. The study allows participants to record their experiences at their own leisure. Equally important, it allows you to view participants' recordings in real-time or in your own time, using various programs created specifically for this.

This activity can be helpful when:

- You are interested in the micro-moments and interactions that affect the "big decision".
- You want to see a variety of experiences and learn how behavior or perception changes according to the environment.
- You worry that direct observers may influence behavior.
- If the activity you are trying to understand is more private, sensitive, or difficult to talk about, having a "barrier" between the researcher and the participant can promote greater transparency.

To do a Diary Study, you will need

1) Define the task and objective.
2) Define conditions for participants: precisely what, when, and how they should take notes, what the triggers should be and how they will provide you with the results.
3) Choose an online or offline option, and limit time.
4) Process the results.
5) The diary can be kept in different formats:
   - In free form, then it is similar to the personal diaries that some people already keep.
   - A structured or closed diary is more like a survey with closed questions in pre-set forms.

Formats of recording conditions

- The filling of the diary can depend **on the intervals** - entries are regular at predetermined time intervals (for example, every 6 hours, once a day, one entry per week, etc.).
- The diary can be filled **by a signal** - with the help of an alert, a call, a text message, or another sign, the organizers or an automatic system will remind you that you need to make a record or answer specific questions.
- The diary can be **event-dependent** - we ask the participant to fill in their diary every time something specific happens (after using your product, after shopping online, when it starts to rain, etc.).

Diaries are less often used as a research activity because of their complexity and length. When choosing a diary study, you should think about all the processes and choose participants who will actually comply with the conditions, especially if the activity is planned for a relatively long period of time.

Topic 5.11: Focus Group

A focus group is a moderated conversation with a group of 5 to 10 participants, during which the moderator offers the group a set of questions on a specific topic. Such groups can be valuable tools for studying attitudes, beliefs, desires, and reactions to concepts or projects. Focus groups usually last between 1 and 2 hours.

Because of their social dimension, focus groups can sometimes elicit spontaneous reactions or ideas more effectively than 1:1 methods such as user surveys. However, there is a risk that participants may influence each other or prevent others from sharing honest opinions or feedback.

Focus groups are helpful when you need to:
- Define or specify research questions at the first stages of the research project.
- Form an idea of how people discuss a problem, product, or shared experience in a group setting.
- Learn about users' opinions, attitudes and preferences after they have used the prototype.

How to conduct a focus group

1) Define the task and goal for the research.
2) Create a plan for the meeting and a precise list of questions you want to discuss.
3) Find a comfortable place to hold a meeting (remember that it's a group, not just 1-2-1 as an interview).
4) Invite a group of 5-10 people who have previously passed a screening.
5) Record the meeting, and involve several facilitators to take notes. Each group is relatively small, but aim for 3 to 6 groups, depending on your research requirements.

To write the correct questions in the script for your focus group:
- Do not ask about hypothetical situations; focus on direct (past) experience, perception, and opinion.
- Keep the questions open-ended; yes/no questions can quickly interrupt the conversation.
- Avoid leading questions that hint at a "correct" answer.

A focus group is not just about interview questions. With a focus group, you can conduct various activities that will help you get the information you need. You can even position them as workshops. You can try to design layouts or draw pictures together (as in the crazy 8s workshop), use list-making, card sorting, or an association game, and generate ideas by answering creative questions like "If our product was a person, what would he/she be?"

To analyze the results of the focus group:

1) Draw a seating chart to show where each participant sat during the exercise.
2) Record observations about group dynamics, body language, and other things that may not be apparent from the audio recording or transcript.
3) Write down the key points and themes that emerge from each question.
4) Try tagging and coding notes as you go; this will save your team time and make it easier to identify patterns in the data as they appear.
5) Keep exciting quotes, including who said what and when.

Here are a few tips for analysing:

1. Review your entries after each stage. Because focus group studies provide so much data from so many different people, it's helpful to write a simple report or summary after each session.

2. Analyze the focus group data. Analysis of focus group data involves analyzing each session individually and then reanalyzing these reports in a meta-analysis of key ideas and themes. An example of systematization of topics:
- Likes and dislikes
- Emotional words
- Mental models
- Problems/pain points

- Ideas/opportunities for product changes or improvements.

Topic 5.12: Field research

Field research is the study of users in their specific setting or environment. Sure, you can interview people and conduct surveys to find answers, but if you want to understand what they're actually doing (not what they say they're doing), you should consider accompanying them as they perform tasks.

Field research is useful when:

- You need to see human behavior in a "natural" environment.
- The role and relevance of the social context is essential to you.
- The environment cannot be conceptually recreated.

Conducting field research can help reveal social facts that may not be immediately obvious or that research participants may not be aware of.

How to conduct a field study

Planning

Presupposes preparation and agreement with the participants. You don't necessarily need a specific set of research questions, but you need a list of scenarios or research theses to understand what flow or activity to observe. Sometimes we may be interested in something general, for example, how the working day of a call center operator in a company goes, or vice versa, something quite detailed, a specific situation or problem. In such studies, researchers try to be as inconspicuous as possible.

Direct observation

This field research involves observing users, their behavior, and why. Ideally, test subjects don't care what you're watching and act as if you're not there.

Sometimes it is an arbitrary format, sometimes with minimal moderation of the tasks to be completed.

Topic 5.13: Shadow observation

Research in the format of "shadow" or shadow observation is a type of field research that involves the complete absence of moderation or a plan with which the participants are introduced. During the conduct of such research, the researcher observes the process and behavior of the participants, sometimes asking clarifying questions.

Before the observation begins, participants are interviewed or participate in group discussions to learn more about their needs.

During the follow-up, the "shadow" develops a list of questions that are then asked of the participant when the follow-up is complete.

Some tips for shadow research

1) The "shadow" UX researcher in this approach should have some idea of what they want to learn during the exercise, and ideally, this should be written down in an easy-to-use form.

2) Observations should be recorded as they are made, although care should be taken not to distract from other observations so that behavior can be reconstructed later.

3) Constant shooting should be avoided. Otherwise, the analysis will be complicated.

I suggest developing an observation sheet (a task description form for notes, time, and other details).

All the types of research discussed can be relevant in different cases; always pay attention to your goal, the resources you can attract, the environment, and the factors that can affect the quality of the information obtained.

Topic 5.14: Competitors analysis

Competitive market research focuses on finding and comparing key market indicators that help identify differences between your products and your competitors' services. Comprehensive market research helps create the foundation for an effective sales and marketing strategy to help your company stand out.

Competitive UX analysis focuses primarily on design and interaction, but researchers also examine how business and other aspects affect the overall user experience.

The analysis is carried out to:

- Understand your position in the market.
- Develop a UX strategy and prioritize the design process.
- Learn how competitors solve similar usability problems.
- Learn about failures and how to avoid them.
- Determine the strengths and weaknesses of the competition.
- Learn about trends and innovations.

The company's competitors in the market can be divided into direct and indirect.

Direct competitors

Offer the same products and services in the same market or because it overlaps with your target market. These competitors usually compete on price because their offerings are very similar. Instagram, TikTok, and Snapchat are direct competitors offering similar products for a similar target market. Not all direct competitors will be precisely the same as your product; sometimes, only key features can overlap or even be semi-direct by covering particular modules.

Indirect competitors

They work in the same market but offer different products. Although they have different products, they usually fulfill the exact needs, so the customer chooses one of them. Instagram and LinkedIn are indirect competitors. Although these platforms serve different needs, they compete for users' attention.

How to conduct competitor analysis?

1. Understand your goals.
2. "Find" your competitors.
3. Look for standard features among competitors.
4. Analyze and summarize.

Choose points for comparing competitors according to your task; they can be:
- The competitor's tone and content with which they communicate with users.
- Good and bad traits.
- User feedback, what works well or poorly.
- Waiting/loading time.
- Customer service.
- Design.
- Compliance with standards.

- In some cases, it may be a comparison of the platforms on which the product is used, the critical audience, or the system's features.

How to identify competitors? Start with the questions:

- Who is currently trying to solve this problem?
- How are they trying to solve the problem?
- What is their key differentiator or unique added value for their business and products?
- Has anyone tried to solve this in the past and failed?
- Why did they fail?

A competitor analysis matrix analyses and prioritizes competitors to determine the "key" ones. It is based on the factors of Market Growth and Market Coverage.

Points on the matrix correspond to competitors.

All competitors on it are divided into four types:

1) Applicants are those who entered the market relatively recently or entered the phase of active growth of the audience and other indicators.

2) Leaders are well-known companies with high coverage, growing in the progression.

3) Niche - the product may not be too successful compared to the leaders but may have local advantages.

4) Compelling performers who have already taken their place in the market; they develop rather slowly but have a high level of loyalty from existing users.

The result of competitor analysis depends entirely on the researcher's ability to interpret the information correctly. A well-thought-out competitive UX analysis can provide valuable information that will push you to implement successful design decisions.

Topic 5.15: SWOT

SWOT analysis is a method that looks at the combination of strengths and weaknesses, opportunities, and threats for your company (product).

The primary purpose of a SWOT analysis is to help organizations develop a complete understanding of all the factors involved in making business decisions. After performing a SWOT analysis, you can plan or evaluate new initiatives, review internal policies, and consider opportunities to change direction or functionality.

A SWOT analysis is designed to facilitate a realistic, fact- and data-based view of the strengths and weaknesses of an organization, initiative, or industry. The organization must maintain analytical precision by avoiding preconceived beliefs or gray areas and focusing on real-life contexts. Companies should use SWOT as a guide, not necessarily as a recipe.

SWOT analysis is used to

- Understand the business context of the company or product.

- Identify gaps in the market and potential problems that need to be solved.

- Uncover market trends that can help you to develop your product definition and understand your company's internal weaknesses and external threats and how to turn them into opportunities.

To conduct a SWOT analysis:

Complete the 4 SWOT categories by conducting in-depth research, gathering information on the Internet, and formulating hypotheses based on them.
OR
Conduct a SWOT analysis of your existing (potential) product and the products of 1-2 of your main competitors, and compare them. If the

competitors are large well-known companies, their SWOT analysis can often be found on the Internet.

A SWOT analysis will give you an overall picture of the company's direction internally and externally. While a SWOT analysis alone won't help you identify the exact problem to solve, it will provide valuable context.

There are four factors in the SWOT analysis table (illustration 11). Internal factors are product strengths and weaknesses. External factors are opportunities and threats.

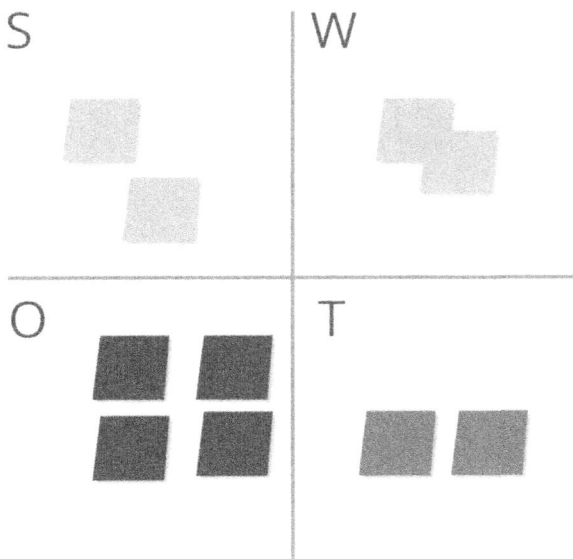

Illustration 11: SWOT Analysis

Strengths

Internal factors positively affect the company, such as knowledge, brand reputation, intellectual property, etc. You can ask questions:
- What do we do well?
- What is our most vital asset?

Weak sides

Internal factors negatively affect the company, such as low financing, low product quality, poor customer service, etc. We ask:
- Which features do our users think work the worst?
- Which of our products is the least effective?

Opportunities

External factors can potentially positively affect the company, such as the acquisition of competitors, significant market growth, international presence, etc. A question for opportunities:
- What trends are evident in the market?
- What demographic groups are we not targeting?

Threats

External factors, such as government regulations, new competitors, and economic downturns, could adversely affect the company. Question:
- How many competitors are there, and what is their market share?
- Are there new regulations that could harm our business or products?

SWOT analysis makes complex problems more manageable. This can require considerable data to analyze and relevant points to consider when making a complex decision. A SWOT analysis that has been prepared by cutting down all the ideas and ranking the items in order of importance will consolidate a significant, potentially overwhelming problem into a more understandable report.

A SWOT analysis requires external analysis. Too often, a company can be tempted to consider only internal factors when making decisions. However, elements beyond a company's control can affect the outcome of a business decision. A SWOT analysis covers internal factors that a company can control and external factors that may be more difficult or impossible to control.

Topic 5.16: Hypothesis validation

Hypotheses are testable assumptions. Assumptions are what we believe to be accurate or what we expect to be true. A hypothesis will be based on what we think we know and our personal experiences or individual perspectives. Assumptions will often turn out to be wrong or at least partially wrong. This is fine as long as we are clear about our assumptions.

Discovery may begin with a problem statement (a plan to create a product or an existing product or service. It may also begin with a set of ideas, a future vision, or a proposition to implement a combination of new business and service models. All of these areas will mean that there are essential assumptions for verification.

In summary, hypothesis generation helps you to develop new ideas about what you need to change. You can do this by sitting in a room brainstorming new features, but connecting with and learning from users is a much faster way to get the data you need.

Structure of hypothesis

- We believe that [something] is true...
- We think [something] is going to happen...
- That's why we think [it] is happening...
- That's what we think creates [this] opportunity...

The hypothesis formula can start with the following:

- We believe that...
- To make sure of this, we...
- To measure this, we can...
- We are right if...

Sometimes, statistical analysts test a hypothesis by measuring and examining a random sample of the analyzed population. Often, designers and analysts can use more than one but several ideas: the null hypothesis and the alternative hypothesis.

The null hypothesis is usually the hypothesis of equality between population parameters; for example, the null hypothesis might state that the average return on a product is not zero. Or in the language of design, for example, users will be satisfied with a specific function. The alternative hypothesis is the opposite of the null hypothesis (for example, the average return is zero), or users will not be satisfied. Thus, they are mutually exclusive, and only one can be true.

The assumption-based approach assumes that we do not perceive information as concrete facts but consider them as assumptions that require verification.

The components of this approach are:

- Key questions we need to answer to learn about these assumptions.

- The people we need to talk to about these assumptions and where we can find them.
- Needs we believe these people have in relation to our product/service/field.

Some examples of hypotheses

"Small e-commerce businesses from Poland will use our development tool." - this hypothesis determines: who - small e-commerce businesses and what - use our tool.

Another example is, "Users can go through all the onboarding steps (onboarding is the initial process with introductory information for new program users)."

Why do hypotheses as a phenomenon work?

Primarily because they help the business deal with possible risks, they are not a 100% guarantee, but they are much better than just a guess from the customer or the team. The second detail is that the approach is based on evidence; not all of them will have the same strength; they can vary from very weak/flimsy evidence to solid and even irrefutable evidence. But again, having evidence is better than mere speculation, even if experienced professionals created it.

Any hypothesis needs to be validated, even if it seems simple and obvious. When choosing a study, you should understand whether you are creating hypotheses or confirming them. Want to understand why no one is registering on your site? Generate some hypotheses by observing users. Do you want to see if mockups will improve your new sign-up process? Test your hypothesis by directly testing the prototype.

Steps for hypothesis validation:

1) Define your main hypotheses. Assumptions can be anything, but if there are too many, prioritize and consider the ones that will have the most impact if you are wrong.

2) Create a prototype. Figure out the most minor, cheapest thing you can build to test this assumption. You can do this in the form of a prototype, an experiment, drawings, or something else to test a hypothesis. Sometimes it's enough to talk to users and collect quantitative data to test an assumption.

3) Experiment. Select users and conduct testing, ask questions, and watch what happens.

4) At the end, analyze the results. Did you confirm your guess? If so, great! Let's go further. If not, analyze and repeat.

A key goal of early-stage product validation work is to provide confidence that you're building the right thing.

As you progress from this early stage to testing the fit of the product or hypothesis, you will engage in analytics. This quantitative data shows exactly how people use that feature or application. This will be the final test to confirm or reject the hypotheses.

Topic 5.18: Contextual inquiry

Contextual inquiry is ethnographic field research involving in-depth observation and interviews with a small sample of users to understand work practices and behaviors clearly. It is often used as an activity to gather information or identify specific details before creating a user experience map.

Context: The research takes place in users' natural environment as they go about their activities normally.

Inquiry: This is the researcher's observation of how a user performs a task and the request for information to understand how and why users do what they do. Sometimes supplemented by a survey or other types of research.

Module 6: UX workshops

Topic 6.1: What are the workshops

UX workshops are intensive collaborative sessions used to problem solve and ensure progress on a specific task throughout development. Workshops allow participants to come together for a focused time, generating ideas and hands-on activities to enable them to achieve their goals.

How does a workshop differ from a regular meeting?

Goal While meetings are a way of sharing information between team members, a workshop is a method of solving a problem, developing a plan, or making a decision.	**Structure** Meetings are often passive (i.e. participants listen and absorb), while workshops encourage active participation.
Scale Meetings tend to allow for superficial coverage of many issues, while workshops are best suited for in-depth, focused coverage of a single issue.	**Duration** Meetings are usually measured in half-hours or hours, while workshops are measured in half-days or days.

There is an extensive list of various activities that are planned as a workshop from the very beginning. They can be scaled, combined, or adapted to be more efficient or meet specific UX challenges. The duration of each session may also vary depending on project needs, scope, and availability of stakeholders.

Q: When is it appropriate to hold workshops?

A: When their value exceeds their price.

Q: When only a shared vision is optimal.

A: When they are clearly facilitated.

When planning a workshop, please pay attention to the goal or task it is supposed to solve, as it can often be quite a costly activity, and preparation is essential.

A workshop is costly, considering various factors, from preparation, materials, and resources to how many people need to be involved. Before conducting it, ensure that you clearly understand your goal and what you want to get as a result, and - if the value exceeds the price - organize. Some activities can be performed independently, so an alternative to workshops can be holding regular meetings, approximately for an hour, for an introductory discussion or information gathering, after which the UX designer can independently process the results and conduct activities individually. But there are situations when the tasks or tasks facing the workshop organizers cannot be parallelized. That is, holding four meetings of 2 hours will not replace one meeting for 8. For such tasks, only a joint vision is optimal, and attempts to do it individually will only be a waste of time.

The facilitator's participation is an essential role in any process of working with workshops. Before its appointment, you need to clearly understand the expected result and all the activities that will be carried out and be able to organize them correctly. Workshops are primarily their planning, considering that time is limited, and the people who will participate often need to become more familiar with the principles of their implementation.

Topic 6.2: Classification of workshops

At the stage of planning workshops, we need to understand what critical task we are pursuing; this will help us choose appropriate activities. There are many types of workshops, and each has specific goals, input information that is needed, and an expected result. We will group them into five categories based on their vital purpose:

1) **Discovery Workshop:** Basic research and consensus on significant milestones and plans for the product. They usually occur at the beginning of the project or at a particular stage of it and help the team form a shared vision and set goals for the product and the project.

2) **Empathy Workshop:** Helps the wider team or stakeholders understand and prioritize user needs before developing a solution. The general approach to empathy is the development of compassion. The workshops are designed so that we empathize and take on the user's role, thereby better understanding his pains and needs.

3) **Design workshop:** allows you to quickly generate and discuss a wide range of ideas with a diverse group of participants. These may include activities for idea generation, collective prototyping, and basic validation of solutions.

4) **Prioritization Workshops:** Used to build consensus on which features customers (or other stakeholders) value most and prioritize them. The very essence of these workshops is made on the prioritization activities we mentioned earlier.

5) **Feedback and Design Critique Workshops:** Used to test design solutions, discussion, and validation, may combine testing or other user-oriented activities.

Discovery Workshop

The workshop's purpose is to reach a consensus on the tasks and plans of the project. Discovery workshops can be a valuable tool to help UX professionals to:
- Understand the business requirements at the start of the initiative.
- Collect existing knowledge from customer teams or stakeholders.
- Build consensus on plans and priorities for the project.

The activities we will choose should be focused on communication and information processing and may include the following:
- Interviews with stakeholders or customers, planning.
- Collection of requirements and their specification.
- Definition of project goals.
- Prioritization of tasks and activities for a specific time.
- Review or creation a roadmap for the project.

Empathy workshop

An empathy workshop aims to help teams or stakeholders understand and prioritize user needs before developing a solution.

Such workshops are used for:
- Defining and sharing a common understanding of who the relevant customers or users are.
- Gaining consensus on user needs, motivations, and behaviors.
- Developing empathy for users.

We can conduct the following:
- Analysis of user research results.
- Create empathy maps.
- Organize discussions and generate suggestions for improvement based on user interviews.
- And other.

Design workshop

This is a broader concept; their purpose is to generate and discuss a wide range of ideas quickly.

They are used most often for:
- Generating ideas, such as drawing, to stimulate discussion.
- Incorporating an interdisciplinary perspective, team discussion, and validation.
- Creating a shared vision as we invite others to co-create.
- Aligning team.

We can apply a variety of techniques, from superficial discussion of ideas to literally creating designs, for example:
- Collaborative design involves the involvement of the entire team, regardless of specialization, and sometimes even potential users in creating certain concepts or system modules.
- Brainstorming, generation of ideas.
- Creation and validation of flows or wireframes.
- Analysis and discussion of visual style.
- Formation of hypotheses.
- And other activities.

Prioritization workshops

In workshops on prioritisation, you are already familiar with the concept.

The purpose of prioritization is to reach a consensus on which features customers (or other stakeholders) value most and prioritize them.

Such workshops are used for:

- Clarification and ranking of the function or idea.
- Creating a focus on certain propositions or concepts.
- Reaching a consensus on which goals, ideas, or user groups to prioritize.
- Choice of solutions.

Some people might argue with the definition of prioritization workshop as a type of workshop and not an activity. Typically because we can address it as an instrument. Most often used for:

- Prioritization of tasks by sprint, quarter, month, etc.
- Discussion and prioritization of assumptions or possible solutions.
- Building a roadmap or other mapping activities where priorities are important.
- And other.

Design feedback or critique workshops

Workshops on feedback and design criticism can be of two types, intra-team (designers, technical specialists, analysts) and at the product level. Intra-team meetings are usually intermediate meetings where specific layouts or solutions are discussed, and ideas for improvement are generated. There are a few cases where this type of workshop can be done at the product level; in that case, the audience is more comprehensive. We attract customers, stakeholders, and users and discuss higher fidelity options.

The goal is to provide space in our design process for design solutions to meet user needs.

Critique workshops can be a valuable tool in helping teams to:
- Evaluations of existing content or designs based on user needs.
- For quick identification of optimal solutions for optimization.
- Planning and validation of long-term solutions for support and optimization.
- Design critique as Testing with users or team members.
- Verifying compliance of the created product or prototype with requirements and success criteria can also be checked.

Here is a short list of activities and techniques you can use:

To form a problem statement:	For voting, communication and decision making:	To generate ideas
How Might We	Dot Voting	Lightning Demos
Expert Interviews	Heat Map	The Four-Step Sketch
The Sailboat	Affinity diagrams	Crazy 8s
The Map	Storyboarding	
Empathy Mapping	Breadboarding Effort/	
Draw Toast	Impact Scale Roadmap	
The 5 Why's	Turn Ideas into Actions	
	Action Board Workshop	

When choosing an activity, focus on five characteristics:

- **Time** (this may include preparation time, execution time, and time to process results).

- **Resources** (in many cases, a workshop requires quite a bit, an online board or a clean wall, stickers, and markers, but some require a whole list).

- **People** (take into account which is needed and whether you have the opportunity to attract them).

- **Input information** (are we working from scratch, is it necessary to conduct several studies before the implementation).

- **Result** (what we get, how to process it, and how to apply it).

I also recommend considering the negative options for the development of events; what will you do if the workshop does not give the expected result? Can you still apply it somehow?

Topic 6.3: Preparing UX workshop

Speaking about preparation for workshops, it should be noted that only some universal models will fit all types. Therefore we will talk about a specific skeleton on which you can adapt the preparation process for any workshop.

Step 1 - Goal

The first step before conducting a workshop is to define the impact we want to create in the organization and determine the available resources (people, tools, time) that we can use to achieve it. Resources are often the driving force at this stage, as some activities can be expensive and time-consuming.

It is necessary to understand very clearly what we want to do and why and how we can further use it.

A common mistake many teams make is to start with an activity (for example, let's make a design sprint!) before considering the results and impact that activity should bring.

Examples of goals can be:

1) Goals from a business perspective:

- Increase in total income.
- Reduction of operating costs.
- Increase in income from new/existing business.

2) Goals from a product perspective:

- Hypothesis testing.
- Definition of X, Y…
- Generation of ideas to solve the problem XYZ.

Step 2 – Activities

Once you've identified your desired impact, you can better define how the workshop can help you figure out the in-betweens – actions, outcomes, and deliverables.

Depending on your questions and gaps in your understanding of the problem and solution space, you will choose which exercises will help you move the project forward.

Workshop activities can be divided based on the goal and question for teams to answer. For example, if our task is to find a solution we would definitely involve some brainstorming activities, or those that help us understand the core of the problem and other factors to really find the most suitable solution. On the other hand, if our goal is keener on understanding the module (area, function, flow, user conditions, etc) we won't go into any brainstorming and prototyping but will focus on the research and team aligning activities, involving empathy and a user-centric approach.

Step 3 – Participants

Due to organizational policies and departmental diversity, there is no magic formula to determine who should participate in a workshop.

However, in most cases, you need:

- Someone who knows about the customer's problems: employees of the registration department, call center, or any other department that understands the problems and pain points of the customers.
- Someone who knows the business: top managers, business analysts, product managers, or anyone else with enough information about how the business makes money and what the company's long-term vision is.
- Someone who understands technology: developers, engineers, data scientists, or anyone else who can provide insight into what is technically possible and what is not.
- Someone who is a local expert on your issue: a specialist who has a deep understanding of the industry, terminology, power user needs, limitations, or other nuances of the tasks they perform.

Step 4 – Logistics

Calculate and plan the details related to the place and time of the event. Book a room or co-working space where everyone can stay. Prepare materials or templates if you are facilitating the workshop remotely. Also, prepare water and snacks if the appointment lasts 2 hours. Check the equipment you need or reserve an additional one.

Prepare a detailed timing of the meeting, taking into account the planned activities. Remember the breaks. A typical rule is a 15-minute break every 2 hours of the workshop. If you have a full 8-hour day, take a 1-hour lunch break and 2-3 15-minute coffee breaks.

Necessary: Make sure everyone has confirmed their participation via email or calendar.

In most cases, it is considered an excellent tone to send the meeting plan with timing and description of activities 24 hours before it so that all participants can familiarize themselves with it and prepare additionally if necessary.

Step 5 – Implementation

Proper facilitation determines the success of the workshop. Start with the desired result. – "By the end of the session, we will do…" or "Our goal is.." is a great way to start the workshop and clearly outline the topics you will be working on to avoid procrastination.

Use icebreakers. In many cases, the participants do not know each other; this will help them work more efficiently and, to a certain extent, energize the atmosphere. Tell the group about the basic rules. They can relate to the order of communication, conducting activities, subordination, etc. Do everything gradually.

This is a structured plan for preparing for workshops. By planning your activities this way, you will be able to design and anticipate most of the aspects you need. Then it's just a matter of the facilitator and the team.

Topic 6.4: Facilitation of workshops

The role of the facilitator is often used in many UX activities. It can be tied to active participation, organization, or moderation of what happens during the workshop.

Facilitation aims to enable and help others achieve their goals, solve critical problems, promote cross-functional collaboration among team members, and encourage innovative problem-solving.

Facilitation applies to workshops, meetings, interviews, focus groups, and other UX activities.

The facilitator takes responsibility for organizing and conducting the meeting, so the team succeeds.

What skills a facilitator needs to develop:

- Active listening - often, the person who facilitates does not take an active part in the process itself because it is essential for him to control many different details. By developing active listening, you will improve your communication skills.

- Empathy is critical in certain types of workshops and, in general, to improve communication. An example of a case when you need compassion may be the beginning of a workshop for a new team; many people may not understand what is happening and what needs to be done; it's your job to find out before everything turns into a pun and help them.

- Diplomacy - conflicts are not rare in workshops; sometimes, a team can work in one direction, and in other cases, it can be several smaller groups supporting different directions of ideas. Conflicts take time, so it's your job to deal with them.

- Objectivity - by objectivity, I mean many concepts, for example, equal treatment of all team members and the ideas they offer, the opinions of performers are not worse than the opinions of customers only because of the hierarchy in the company, being objective you are a particular referee in case of misunderstandings.
- Punctuality - one of the critical tasks is maintaining timing. Workshops are expensive, so the team cannot afford to waste time on extraneous issues.

Depending on the type of workshop you will be facilitating, you may have different tasks, such as:

- Organization of the meeting.
- Holding a meeting.
- Tracking time and timing and ensuring compliance with the schedule.
- Settlement and resolution of disputes.
- Summing up.

Depending on the type of workshop or team you will be working with, you may be:

- Energizer: to encourage people to think creatively and participate.
- Driver: keep everyone on schedule and maintain progress.
- A diplomat: to create trust, goodwill, and cooperation in the group.
- An interpreter: to reveal hidden connections and communicate with an eye on the big picture.

Important to understand that facilitation is not only about the organization or making everyone comfortable and inspired, it's about process and result. And your goal, as a facilitator, is to help other team members to succeed. So choose the methods that help you align the team, and make the expected outcome more realistic and qualitative.

A few tips

1) When creating a meeting plan, allow enough time for intros and room for small talk.

2) Plan the minimum and maximum activities you want to do, where "minimum" will define the minimum amount of actions needed for the workshop to be successful.

3) A facilitator is not a clown. Any entertainment for the team is done only to ensure a high collective result and should not go beyond the scope of the work process. The facilitator charges and directs the team, but subordination and a severe attitude must be maintained throughout the work.

The facilitator is also usually involved in planning the processes and schedule of each workshop; for this, use estimation techniques to estimate the possible duration of the task.

Topic 6.5: Icebreaking

Icebreakers and team-building techniques warm everyone up before the workshop, help to create the right mindset, create positive energy, develop empathy for teammates, and add context to your day-to-day work.

It is usually not an extended activity, up to 15 minutes, which helps everyone get involved and get to know each other. Often this is a verbal activity, but sometimes it also involves a moving component.

Cool icebreaker:

- Involves everyone and everything.

- Non-standard and not directly related to the product or topic of the workshop.
- With a light touch of comedy.

Depending on what you will do, icebreakers can be of 3 types:

1) To get to know each other, for example, we can ask everyone to introduce themselves or tell an interesting fact about themselves.

2) To rally the team to a specific action: this type involves the team being given some small joint task and having to complete it in a short time, usually something straightforward but should involve everyone.

3) Icebreakers, emphasizing physical activities, are often used when we need to encourage participants not to be passive but to participate actively.

Module 7: Ideation

Topic 7.1: Generating ideas

As a creative process, **ideation is a set of methods, activities, and events that help us work with a solution for a given task.** Participants gather with open minds to generate as many ideas as possible to solve a problem in a non-judgmental environment. Before you start brainstorming, your team needs a well-defined problem – a focused problem statement or point of view (POV) that we should have after conducting the activities of the previous stages; we will also have validated assumptions, specific ideas, research results, etc. And now, let's talk about the generation of ideas as a phenomenon.

The idea helps:

- Asking the right questions and innovating by focusing on your users, their needs, and what you think about them.
- Go beyond obvious solutions and, therefore, increase the innovative potential of your solution.
- Bring together the perspectives and strengths of your team members.

Rules for generating ideas

1) Generation is aimed at quantity, not quality. By focusing on getting as many ideas as possible, people are more willing to share things they might otherwise write off as irrelevant or redundant.

2) You want people to think big. This encourages more creative thinking because people know they are not only allowed but encouraged to think outside the box.

3) This stage is not a critique of ideas on the spot - it's just generation. The lack of immediate feedback allows people to share ideas more openly without fear of failure or disapproval.

4) There is a concept called "sharing". Although criticism is not allowed, brainstorming participants can draw on other people's input. This creates a more collaborative atmosphere where good ideas get even more support.

The brainstorming environment promotes a free flow of ideas, concepts, solutions, and strategies without judgment. In brainstorming, all contributions are valid, and the key to a successful session is to share as many ideas as possible without judging them.

What do you need to get started?

1) A clearly defined and formulated problem will be addressed during the session.

2) A facilitator is a person who can manage and moderate the process.

3) The required number of people (not too large, not too small, for an even distribution of work among group members, typically this number is similar to the scrum team, i.e., 7 participants, plus or minus two, but there are situations when even two people can form a powerful team).

As Don Norman explains in Rethinking Design Thinking, ideas are critical in making us question the obvious, challenge the norm, and come up with new ideas: "It is by questioning the obvious that we make great progress. This is where breakthroughs come from. We need to question the obvious, reframe our beliefs and rethink existing solutions, approaches, and beliefs."

Topic 7.2: Tools and methods for generating ideas

Walt Disney method

Walt Disney is known all over the world for his creative work. How he developed creative and innovative ideas is described in The Walt Disney Method. The team considers three different perspectives: Dreamer, Realist or Creator, and Critic.

Number of participants: 3-9 (12).

Time: from 30 minutes to 2 hours.

The goal is to try to solve the problem using three different approaches:

1) Dreamer. He does not think that everything is impossible. Instead, he thinks about fantasy.

2) Realist/Creator. He does not think too much but immediately starts working step by step.

3) Critic. Questions everything and looks for contradictions and what might happen in the future.

The team either moves through all three points of view together, in turn or splits between roles to allow discussion between different parties.

The Walt Disney Method begins with the dreamer's point of view. At this stage, the goal is to write down what is (technically) possible or even realistic. All crazy ideas are allowed, and in no case should not be hindered by possible risks; we try to open our thinking as much as possible, but we do not go into the topic of "flying ponies and unicorns"; try to be precise. The general position of any brainstorming is openness and unlimitedness. As dreamers, we could come up with something extraordinary, but even when we set ourselves the goal of opening all the "boundaries", it motivates us; there are cases when it can be a particular burden and take away too much time.

After some ideas have been found and expanded from the dreamer's point of view, it is possible to move on to the following perspective. The Realist/Creator is in direct contrast to the Dreamer's views. At this stage, the team considers which ideas are helpful or enrich the product. What materials will be needed for implementation, or what difficulties might the idea or concept cause?

The critic embodies the criticism and the last view of the team. Previously developed realist approaches are criticized or questioned when trying on this role. Are there risks or gaps in the idea or concept? What needs to be improved?

Reviewing the three points of view is repeated until the critic has no questions left. As a result, we will receive many ideas with different options for their development, and we can vote for those that would best suit our situation. But please note that our goal is not to choose the most realistic and safe options; this is limiting; our goal is to choose those that, after working with, we will get the best results.

Crazy 8s

"Crazy eights" is the primary design sprint method for brainstorming. This technique is best used when ideas should come faster during the ideation stage because you have data to build on.

The goal is to generate several different ideas in a short period of time. You should get one or more ideas that can be turned into a prototype. To find the best answer or solution to your initial question or problem, testing the idea with real users is essential.

Number of participants: unlimited (but ideally no more than 12 in a group).

Time: about 20 minutes active part, up to 1 hour of discussion.

The peculiarity of crazy eights is the need to generate ideas very quickly. We adjust to the fact that we need to get a result, not one, but 8. The brain activates, and even if many of these ideas may not be applicable, some may become genius, even though they were not obvious.

Start with identifying a fundamental problem or task the entire team will work on. Assign someone as a timekeeper, so you are not distracted by the clock. Fold the paper into eight different parts. Set a timer and ask participants to start drawing. The facilitator should prompt them every minute to start a new sketch in the next section. Emphasize that they should not limit themselves. Make sure they get all their ideas out there and approach them open-mindedly. At this stage, it's about the number of ideas, not the quality. It is usual for participants to be in a hurry. It's part of the process. Usually, the active part of this work takes 1 or 2 minutes for each picture, that is, 8 or 16 minutes for all stages. It would be best if you had a collection of ideas when the eight minutes are up. Some are unexpected, some are weird, and some might not work. Each member then presents their top three ideas to the rest of the team for feedback.

Work through the results, determine what went well, and pin them on the board, discuss this idea; you need a discussion. So, as often as it will just be a mountain of lines and unclear elements, the author must present the picture to the team and explain its logic. Further, ideas can be combined, changed, and adapted, but this is another task.

Figure storming

Figure storming is an opportunity to "put yourself in someone else's place" for practice. If there is someone you admire, a celebrity or someone in your field, think about how they would handle the process or what they might come up with. It can help you start your creative journey.

If you're designing a new inclusive smartphone, ask yourself, "What would Steve Jobs do?" Given that he was one of the first to popularize UX in the development company, how would he solve your problem?

When choosing a person to stand in for, choose someone well-known about whom you can easily find more information. It does not necessarily have to be inventors, designers, and engineers. These can be singers, presidents, famous personalities, comedians, scientists, etc. The criterion of success understands the non-standard nature of this character, how he differs from others, and why his opinion would not be the same as everyone else's.

To start, choose a well-known person who is not in the room—this could be a boss, a fictional character, or a prominent public figure—and discuss how that person would approach or think about the problem. (When choosing a character, you can focus on someone related to your field and even introduce him to colleagues in more detail, or on the contrary, choose someone completely different).

Put forward your creative ideas on behalf of the chosen person. Discuss the options. The advantage of this technique is that people are often shy to present their ideas, but it is easier for them when they do it on behalf of another person.

Worst idea in the world

"Worst Possible Idea" or "The worst idea in the world" is an idea generation method where team members purposefully seek out the worst possible solutions during brainstorming sessions.

The flipped search process relaxes them, builds their confidence, and ignites their creativity so they can explore these ideas, challenge their assumptions, and learn about great ideas.

Such a workshop is held in two stages:

1) Participants will offer the worst, in their opinion, ideas for implementing the solution (it can be something wrong, illogical, or unrealistic).

2) Participants then discuss and analyze these solutions and try to extract possible improvements from these ideas.

Often we are so fixated on the fact that we need to find the right solution, preferably not expensive and convenient, both for the user and for the business, that we need to remember that the critical goal of the idea generation process is actually generated. We don't need one because we won't find the perfect one immediately. We need those who help us form a scope to work with it. The same method makes the task somewhat more accessible and relaxes us. Because by looking for bad ideas instead of good ones, we start generating them, as they should be, rather than evaluating them immediately.

Topic 7.3: Working with ideas

Prioritization is one of the culminating activities performed during or after any workshop.

Prioritization can be carried out in the following formats:

- Voting: Assumes that everyone on the team has one or more votes to cast on one or more ideas.

- Comparison: involves determining the critical factor of success (or success criteria), and checking the compliance of various ideas with it.

- Benchmarking: This is a complex matrix system that involves defining a list of suitability criteria (for example, realism, cost, effort, etc.) and evaluating all options against them.

Prioritization is aimed not only at a superficial determination of the best idea or proposal but also at a specific comparison of factors, for contrast, to confirm why it could be or is better.

Dot voting

In dot voting, each person in the group is given a certain number of tokens ("dots"), each of which can be assigned to an alternative that is part of a set of other options.

This voting tool is used when:

- It would be best if you focused your discussion on a subset of the alternatives in the more extensive set.
- The conversation around the final decision is full of conflict and anxiety.
- Different points of view are needed, but only a few opinions are heard.
- If you have to make quick group decisions in a short period of time.

This method is helpful because it prevents the HIPPO effect and allows all participants to contribute equally. **The HIPPO effect is that the opinion of the highest-paid person is considered more in the decision-making because it has a higher value.** Thus, the matter of an idea is related to the salary or status in the company of the person expressing the opinion. The higher the salary, the more critical the thought. However, this is not always optimal because the "importance" of an idea is not proportional to its correctness, so voting with dots rejects the HIPPO effect and equalizes everyone.

Voting can have different initial rules. Usually, depending on the task, each participant receives 1, 2, or 3 votes, which he can give for one or more ideas that he considers the best. However, there can be gradation; although the method fights against the HIPPO effect, sometimes certain team members can be given more votes; for example, the facilitator, who usually does not actively participate in the generation of ideas, is the most unbiased because his options are not among the total number.

Prioritization by parameters

Typically, similar to what you would do for prioritizing tasks in a scope, prioritization of ideas can also be started from a matrix, which allows you to compare and evaluate arguments according to various parameters and a defined scale. The parameters are chosen arbitrarily according to the needs of the project. We can compare by finances, impact on users or business, complexity, etc.

As an example, consider the assessment of options according to the following parameters:

- Compliance with user needs (on a scale where one is low compliance, 5 = five is full compliance).

- Compliance with business needs (where one is low, five is full compliance).

- Technical capabilities (where one is almost unreal, five is real).

- Technical complexity (where one is tricky, five is effortless).

To carry out such prioritization, first, select the criteria. They can be different for each situation, so you need to pay attention to your limitations, general requirements, etc. Also, when choosing standards that are more technical or business-related, make sure that prioritization involves representatives from the production team and the business, who can more objectively evaluate the ideas. With the scale, you will also need to work individually, as sometimes it will have to be inverted. The general principle is the highest cumulative score, that is, for a particular idea or proposal to gain more points, so the highest score in the scale you choose should be the best positive result. Next, after evaluating all the ideas according to the parameters on the proposed scales, you sum up the values of all alternatives and compare them. There are cases when a uniform estimate could be more optimal; for example, if we are working on innovation, we immediately understand that the technical complexity will be relatively low, which will mean a rather complex implementation. However, by consciously choosing a problematic implementation, we want to be sure that users will be satisfied. Therefore, to make the difference in ideas more tangible, we can add a coefficient to the value of user satisfaction. Thus, comparing a complex task with a less complex one, but on the condition that the complex one has a higher level of happiness, we will choose the more complex one. And mathematics will explain this because even if some tasks are a little easier to implement, user satisfaction will be lower. The total score for prioritization will also be lower since happiness has a greater weight.

Other methods

- The Effort / Impact matrix is a classic option, which we have already mentioned.
- The Effort / Urgency matrix - this variation compares effort and urgency. The principle is similar to the Eisenhower matrix; the priority is what is urgent and not complex, what is critical but challenging, and what is not urgent. The concept of urgency is relative, and the team can assess what exactly and in comparison with what is urgent. For example, it may be urgent because there is a system bug ruining the user experience, and it needs to be fixed

quickly. Or, it may be urgent because the discount season is approaching and we would like to increase sales by introducing new features.

- The Risk / Value matrix is another variation of the matrix that considers risks and value. In other words, we ask the question, "If we complete this task, design an idea, or present an innovation to a user, what are the risks? The concept of risk is also relative and will differ from project to project. For example, it can be a time risk and a comparison of the probability that after choosing a particular idea, we will not implement it on time, or a risk in terms of complexity, what is the probability that we will not succeed in doing it, etc.

- Prioritization by success criteria is a subjective option based on our success criteria and compares ideas for compliance with a conditional scale that we define for each case separately. For example, we can rank, that is, evaluate the correspondence of ideas to the criterion of success, and set them in order from the most appropriate to the least, or define a certain threshold, that is, the threshold of correspondence in percentages, and discard all options whose assessment is lower than this level. As a result, we will get an order of the ideas that were compared, where the first idea will fully or most meet the success criterion, and the last one in the list will be the least or not at all.

- Prioritization by "Must, Should, Could, Won't" involves more sorting than prioritization. It has four priorities defined as alternatives or columns in the table; the first determines that we must do it, the second that we should do it, the third that we could do it, and the fourth that we should not or will not do it. Each idea during this prioritization will receive its letter M, S, C, or W, and prioritization will continue in the middle of each group.

Module 8: Working with a solution

Topic 8.1: Information architecture

Information architecture is a discipline that focuses on organizing information in digital products. IA allows you to plan the exact placement and combination of various pages and a flow that allows users to move between screens without much effort.

Although IA is not actually visible to end users, it is at the heart of the design. An information architect's job is to create an experience that allows the user to focus on their tasks rather than finding their way around.

Factors that should be taken into account when creating IA:

1) Gestalt principles, which we have already mentioned, explore the visual perception of objects about each other, including similarity, continuity, proximity, symmetry, and closure.

2) Mental models are assumptions that people have in their minds before they interact with a product. For example, when a user is looking for contact information, the first thing they will look for is a page, link, or section that says "Contact Us" or "Contact" in this case, not only will the placement be necessary, but also the literal word or the phrase we will use for the title. For example, "Contact" is unambiguous, but "About us", or "Write to us, is somewhat more ambiguous.

3) Cognitive load is the mental effort the user must put into interacting with the product. In the context of information architecture design, cognitive load is the amount of information a user can process at any given time.

For creating IA, we need the following:

1) Start with User Research. Excellent product design starts with thorough user research. Researching what users need and want is critical to creating effective IA design. These can be:
- Interviews with users.
- Card sorting and tree testing sessions.
- Usability testing.
- Contextual inquiries and research.

2) The next activity that can be used to create IA is Content Inventory, Grouping, and Content Audit. Information architects must have a good understanding of the content offered by the product. Content inventory, grouping, and validation help UX architects achieve this.

3) Viewing Taxonomy and Labeling. **Taxonomy is the practice of organizing and classifying items based on similarities. This exercise typically follows user research and content inventory processes.** IA can categorize items using categories, sections, or metadata tags. During this process, it is essential to remember that the content and functionality of the product will expand, so the way it is organized must be easily scalable.

We can include here:
- Creation hierarchy and navigation.
- Labeling, i.e., defining names for menu items or pages.
- Prototyping to test assumptions using words, etc.

160

Eight principles of information architecture creation

The principle of objects: content should be treated as a living, breathing entity. It has lifecycles, behaviors, and attributes. We understand that this is not an independent point; the content must come from somewhere, have connections, and be part of the whole.

Selection principle: less is better. Reduce the number of options to a minimum. People do not perform well when there is too much choice; it increases cognitive load and stress.

Disclosure principle: use information previews to help users understand what information is hidden if they dig deeper. It would be best if you also remembered connections, present what you can get, and record where the user came from.

Principle of samples: show examples of content when describing the range of categories. For instance, in a form where you need to enter data, you can add a model or an input mask to help users better understand what they want.

The principle of the entrance door: assume that at least 50% of users will use an entry point other than the home page. This principle takes that you cannot build an architecture and plan navigation from only one point; by going to any other page, users must understand where they are and be able to navigate the product.

The principle of several classifications offers users several classification schemes for viewing site content. For example, typically, on the site, you can use the top navigation to find the necessary category and the search field, filtering, or other methods.

The principle of focused navigation: keep navigation simple and never mix things up.

The principle of growth (scaling): assume that the content on the website will grow. Make sure the website is scalable. This applies not only to the navigation, whether you will be able to add new categories but also to the content itself and the structure of the layout.

Transparent and understandable IA has a positive effect on the reputation and SEO ranking of search engines Actions to improve the information architecture leads to a reduction in cost, operational assistance, and support documentation, that is, a department or call center where operators will be told how to find something on the site, and this has a positive effect on the use of resources.

Topic 8.2: Navigation models

When creating IA essential to understand not only project and domain specifics but general components and elements for IA. Information architecture covers not only the top or visible navigation; it unites all of the items in the system.

The four main components of IA for web products traditionally include:

- Organization systems - define how we categorize information, such as by topic or chronology.
- Marking systems - how we present information, such as scientific terminology.
- Navigation systems - this is how we view or navigate through information, such as clicking through a hierarchy.
- Search systems - how we search for information, such as performing an index search.

Organization systems

Organizational systems define the methods of organizing information and presenting it to the user. They can be **specific and ambiguous**.

Detailed or specific organization charts divide information into well-defined and mutually exclusive sections. Knowing the person's last name, you can look up that letter in the alphabetical list. This is called a known element search. You know what you're looking for, and it's obvious how to find it. The problem with precise organization schemes is that they require the user to know the specific name of the object they are looking for.

Include:

- Alphabetical by letters in the alphabet.
- Chronological by dates, number of pages, or other numerical values.
- The geographic system, for example, by country of publishing or author's place of birth.

Ambiguous systems of organization and presentation of information to the user cannot be precisely defined. Such systems are difficult to design and maintain and can be challenging.

For example, is a tomato a vegetable or a fruit?

However, structuring options are often more important and useful than precise organizational charts. After all, the search for information is often iterative and interactive.

Ambiguous systems include classification systems according to:

- Topic or subject
- Task
- The audience
- Metaphors

When choosing an organization system, pay attention to your audience. The system is quite individual for each project. For example, an alphabetical or thematic approach is prominent if you create a product designed for information content, such as an online library. Still, when it comes to more specific systems, such as an intranet or a particular functional network, you can use more ambiguous systems, for example, based on the principle of the task.

Marking systems

Determine precisely how a specific navigation object is marked. The two main types used are text or image.

Text labels are the most common labels. Types of text labels include:
- Contextual links - text in the body of a document or a fragment of information, links as we used to call them.
- Headlines - used to establish a hierarchy in the text.
- Parameters of the navigation system.
- Index terms - often called keywords, descriptive metadata, taxonomies, or controlled vocabularies.

Images are most often used as labels in the mobile navigation system. Less often, they can serve as titles. The problem with icon labels (icons) is that they are less informative than text. That's why they were used for a navigation system or a small organization system where the list of options is small. But designing them is still risky because the user can get confused.

Navigation systems

Navigation systems - determine the way of building navigation mechanisms. They are divided into global, local, and unique or point navigations.

A global or site-wide navigation system often complements the information hierarchy by providing more significant vertical and lateral movement throughout the site. Most global navigation systems are based on some standard rules that dictate the implementation of the system at each level of the site.

A more complex website may need to supplement the global navigation system with one or more local navigation systems. To understand the need for local navigation systems, it is necessary to understand the concept of a subsite.

The term "subsite" was coined by Jakob Nielsen to describe a recurring situation where a collection of web pages within a more prominent site invokes a typical style and shared navigation mechanism unique to those pages.

In Custom Navigation, Links between content elements do not always fit neatly into the hierarchical, global, and local navigation categories. An additional category of particular references is more editorial than architectural. Typically, an editor or content specialist determines the appropriate locations for these links after the content is placed in the website architecture.

Consider several types of navigation systems:

- **Hierarchical**. This standard type for content-heavy websites provides users with multiple routes to navigate. In the Toyota example, we can see multiple tabs, but in many cases, this type of navigation will manifest itself through navigation breadcrumbs and other additional navigation options. It usually has too many links and opportunities for smaller objects like the mobile screen, so lately, this navigation is almost exclusively used on desktops.

- **Nested lists.** One of the most common types of mobile navigation is often used to organize multi-level and "heavy" menus. It's also one of the best patterns for responsive design, as it allows you to collapse those above hierarchical tree-like navigation. Users click on items of interest to open additional menus.

- **Bento box.** Named after the Japanese lunch box is a navigation bar that gives you an overview of several pieces of dynamic information. You can view specific parts in more detail if you wish. This is very common in fitness and financial applications where large amounts of data are generated, and the user usually needs an overview.

- **Hubs and transitions.** The name of this model speaks for itself, there is the main screen acts as a hub, and links point to other sections that live independently of each other. The Google Play Store uses this model in its main categories, giving you an easy way to navigate to albums or books you might want to buy. All your attention is drawn to the purchase or download button on the page, so you are not distracted by global navigation or other unnecessary information.

Search systems

The search engine is only effective for products with much information when users risk getting lost. In this case, developers must consider a search engine, filters, and many other tools that help users find content and plan what the data will look like after the search. Search engines allow users to enter search terms into a search bar - just as they would in a search engine like Google - and quickly find the results, they're looking for. It's an excellent choice for websites and apps with many data and various features. To choose a navigation tool, start by choosing a taxonomy.

Taxonomy is the practice and science of classification. Creating a taxonomy is a critical step in creating the structure of your site. In the case of IA, it attempts to group different unstructured pieces of information and give them descriptions to create a more structured design. The most crucial technique for the taxonomy of content is card sorting.

IA should always be formulated with the target user in mind. So once you have your content, conduct a series of card-sorting sessions with your target audience to organize it. The point of the activity is to see how users perceive pieces of website content.

A broad-to-narrow approach to organizing your content is recommended because it aligns well with how people interact with content (general to specific). After establishing the hierarchy, the next step is implementing it in the design. The navigation structure should offer a natural flow of information, which happens when designers choose the right navigation element for each type of content.

Topic 8.3: Card sorting

Card sorting is a method used to design or evaluate the information architecture of a site. During the card sorting session, the participants organize the topics into categories they understand and can also help you label these groups. To perform card sorting, you can use actual cards, pieces of paper, or several online card-sorting software tools.

For card sorting, it's a good idea to recruit members who match the demographics of your intended users. The number of participants depends on the card sorting format.

Why does card sorting work?

Sorting cards will help you understand your users' expectations and understanding of your topics. This is usually very useful when doing deep

research to learn more about your users and understand your content. Knowing how your user group handles information can help you:
- Create the structure of your product.
- Decide what to put on the main page.
- Categorize labels and navigation.
- Card sorting is a reasonably popular method used at the beginning of the information architecture process.

How to sort

1) To get started, choose a set of themes. The group should include 40-80 items (cards) representing the site's main content. Write each topic on a separate card.
2) Shuffle the cards and give them to the participant. Ask the user to look at the cards in turn and arrange the cards that belong to the same group into piles. Some stacks may be significant, others small.
3) When a participant has grouped all the cards, give them blank cards and ask them to write a name for each group they made. This step will reveal the mental model of the user's topic space.
4) And repeat. Conduct an activity with 15-20 participants.

To improve the process and get even more insights to ask additional questions:
- Which items were particularly easy or difficult to place?
- Did any items belong to two or more groups?
- What do you think of the things left unsorted (if any)?

You can also ask the user to think out loud while they perform the original sort. Consider that different users may have different approaches, some will start sorting alphabetically, some by category, and some by type of interaction, simulating workflow. All versions have the right to life and maybe even lead you to a variation with adaptive navigation.

There are several variations of card sorting.

1) **Open Card Sorting** is the most common type. When practitioners use the term card sort, it is meant to be a face-up card sort. When sorting available cards, users can assign any name to the groups they have created with the cards in the stack.

2) **Closed Card Sorting** is where users are given predetermined category names and asked to sort individual cards into those categories. Closed card sorting does not reveal how users conceptualize a set of topics. Instead, it is used to evaluate how well the existing category structure supports the content from the user's perspective.

There is also a third, less popular type; it is a hybrid.

3) **A hybrid Card Sorting** is where you give your members predefined categories, similar to a face-down card sort, but you also allow them to create their categories if they don't find one they like. Researchers use this technique when they already have specific categories but want information from their target customers about others.

Also, by the type of moderation, i.e., sorting support can be moderated or unmoderated.

- **Moderated card sorting** involves the presence of a moderator and additional communication: summarizing (and/or thinking aloud during the actual sorting). This step is a precious opportunity to gain qualitative insight into users' reasoning for their grouping. You can ask questions, explore further understanding and ask about specific cards as needed.

Unmoderated card sorting involves users organizing content into groups independently, usually using an online tool, without interaction with a facilitator. It is generally faster and cheaper than moderated card sorting because it does not require a researcher to talk to each user. Unmoderated card sorting can be helpful as a supplement to moderated card sorting sessions.

Topic 8.4: Customer Journey Map

CJM (customer journey map) can help you, and your product visualises how customers feel at all contact points with the brand. You can avoid potential problems early, increase customer retention and gain critical insights to make the best business decisions. CJM can be an independent artifact closely related to all previous research, persona, etc. Let's consider how to create it.

Customer journey map (customer experience map) - a diagram, flowchart, or illustration of all the touch points between your customers and your company, whether online or offline, defined as a customer journey map. This helps identify where your product is helping customers or holding them back from achieving their goals.

CJM is a popular activity because it:

- Helps change the company's perspective from the inside out.
- Breaks down prejudices and helps create a shared vision for the entire organization.
- Allows you to identify those responsible for key interaction points with the user in internal departments of the company or product.
- Focuses on specific customers. Therefore it specifies, although it still considers different people's characteristics.
- Helps to understand quantitative data.

Outlining your current processes helps to visualize what the customer is experiencing in real-time and can reveal common pain points that need to be addressed.

To create a user experience map:

1) Understand the objectives. Meet business owners or stakeholders to define and agree on all project goals.

2) Define the scope of the business. Scoping the process is critical, helping to determine what research is needed next and letting you know what level of the story is being delivered on CJM.

3) Collect information. Evaluate and explore your data. You need to decide what factor you will take into account to reflect on this journey, your client (persona), and his tasks.

4) When defining a user's goal, you first have a line segment, the two points defining where the user starts and what they want to achieve. You will need to break this path down into steps to achieve it. Journey maps are best suited for scenarios that involve a sequence of events.

5) Create a hypothetical map. To initiate the customer journey process, create a collaborative environment by inviting the Business, Design, and Development teams to better understand the customer's perspective.

6) Start by dividing the user journey into phases. For example: if the user's task is to buy headphones online, the phases can be:

1. Discover - we search for a product, perhaps filter the list, or use other parameters.

2. Try - we find the desired product and familiarize ourselves with its characteristics and functionality.

3. Buy - add to the cart and place an order.

4. Use - we receive the product to use it.

5. Support - this phase can be optional if they need to change or repair the warranty product.

7) Test and update your hypothesis. Instead of giving your customers a long list of questions, contextual inquiry can encourage them to use a product or service as they would typically.

8) Create a visually appealing journey map.

To actions divided into phases, write additional steps or details necessary for the global task, and add Mindset. Mindset can be motivation, quotes from interviews, details, explanations, and additions to actions. We want not only to say what the person is doing but also to explain why. For example, the Mindset at the Discover stage when buying headphones online may include a description of what the person is looking for, search criteria, and methods used.

Next, you need to add the person's emotions, the emotions with which he goes along the way to accomplishing his task. They can be both positive and negative. Emotions are not imaginary criteria, we start from previous studies, and as a result, they can be a factor that will determine the success of the product. For example, suppose we understand that our users are often confused or angry in the Discovery stage. In that case, we can change our assumptions and form new hypotheses that will indicate how we could improve the Discovery process or its settings so that our users are positive in the plan emotions at this stage, or at least neutral.

In the end, we add an "Opportunities" section. The map is not self-sufficient if it only shows the problem points; its real meaning is to find ways to improve (illustration 12).

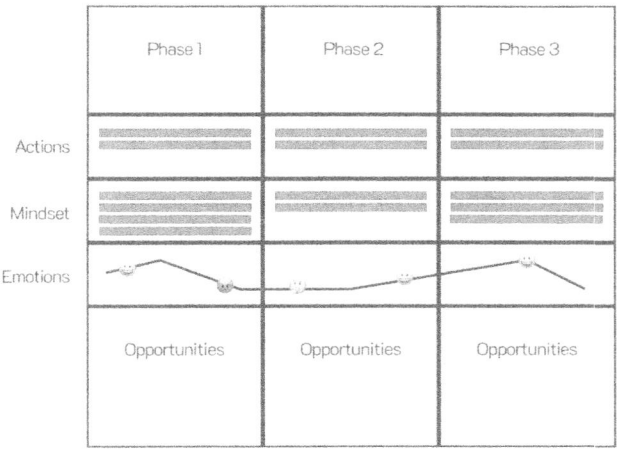

Illustration 12: Skeleton of CJM

One of the most exciting and informative elements of CJM is the points of interaction with customers. They make up the bulk of your customer journey map. It's how and where customers interact with and experience your brand. When you research and plan your touchpoints, include information that addresses action elements, emotions, and potential problems.

A user experience map can be used in two formats. As-is works best; it's a visualization format of the situation at hand that helps us see and identify points for further investigation to improve the product. Another variant of to-be is a variant that defines a somewhat idealized view of the user's path. You can map out components or interaction details that are your goal for the overall experience and will improve existing pain points or design an entirely imaginative fantastic experience. The peculiarity of the to-be map is that it can help to form, visualize and present an idea of a new product, which does not have direct analogs at a particular moment, from another point of view, if you work with an existing product, the to-be map can be only another guess.

173

Topic 8.5: 10 UX rules

UX laws are user experience or phycological laws that explain certain behaviour of the user and help us to target his needs or understand the attitude better.

Here is a short overview of 10 popular and influential UX rules from product and phycology to improve and empower your next project.

Hick's law

Hick's law (or the Hick-Hyman law) is named after the British and American psychologists William Edmund Hick and Ray Hyman. As might be expected, the more stimuli to choose from, the longer it takes the user to decide which one to interact with. Users bombarded with choices must spend time interpreting and making decisions, giving them extra work they don't want.

Hick's Law defines that: the time required to make a decision increases with the number and complexity of choices.

To incorporate the law:

- Minimizing choices when response time is critical to reducing decision time.
- Break complex tasks into smaller steps to reduce cognitive load. For example, as in the onboarding process, if we ask the user to enter much information at once, he probably won't use our product because we ask too much at once, so onboarding is often done in fragments, with 2-3 questions for each step.
- Avoid overwhelming users by highlighting recommended options.
- Use progressive adaptation to minimize cognitive load for new users.
- Be careful not to simplify to the point of abstraction.

Fitts's Law

In 1954, psychologist Paul Fitts, studying the human motor system, showed that the time required to move to a target depends on its distance but is inversely proportional to its size. According to this law, fast movements and small targets lead to more errors due to the trade-off between speed and accuracy. Although there are several variants of Fitts' Law, all capture this idea. Fitts' Law is widely used in user experience (UX) and user interface (UI) design. For example, this law influenced the practice of making interactive buttons large (especially on finger-controlled mobile devices) - pressing smaller buttons is harder and takes longer

Fitts' Law: target detection time depends on the distance and size of the target. Therefore, consider the following:

- Touch targets should be large enough for users to select them accurately.
- There must be sufficient distance between the contact elements.
- Touch objects should be placed in areas of the interface that make them easily accessible.

Jacob's Law

Jacob's Law was created by Jacob Nielsen, a consumer advocate and head of the Nielsen Norman Group, which he co-founded with Dr. Donald A. Norman. Dr. Nielsen pioneered the "discount usability engineering" movement to quickly and cheaply improve user interfaces and invented several usability techniques, including heuristic evaluation.

Jacob's Law: users spend most of their time on other sites. This means that users prefer your site to work like all the other sites they already know.

In work, it is worth considering that

- Users will transfer the expectations they have built around one familiar product to another that looks similar.
- By leveraging existing mental models, we can create a great user experience where users can focus on their tasks instead of learning new models.
- When making changes, minimize friction by allowing users to continue using the standard version for a limited time.

Miller's law

In 1956, George Miller argued that immediate memory and absolute judgment are limited to about seven pieces of information. The basic unit of information is the bit, the amount of data required to choose between two equally likely alternatives. Similarly, 4 bits of information are a decision between 16 binary options (4 consecutive binary decisions).

Miller's Law: the average person can store only 7 (plus or minus 2) items in their working memory. This law is not directly connected to UI principles but allows us to define UX principles and understand how cognitive load impacts the interfaces.

To incorporate the law:

- Don't use the "magic number seven" to justify unnecessary design limitations.
- Organize content into smaller chunks to help users process, understand, and remember efficiently.
- Remember that the amount of short-term memory depends on the person's previous knowledge and the context of the situation.

Proximity Principle

The principles of proximity (or Gestalt laws of grouping) are principles in psychology first proposed by Gestalt psychologists to explain the observation that people naturally perceive objects as organized patterns. Gestalt psychologists argued that these principles exist because the mind has an innate tendency to perceive patterns in stimuli based on specific rules. These principles fall into five categories: proximity, similarity, continuity, closure, and connectedness.

Proximity Principle: objects close to each other tend to group together.

- Proximity helps establish a connection with nearby objects.
- Elements located in close proximity are perceived as having similar functions or features.
- Proximity helps users understand and organize information faster and more efficiently.

Pareto's Principle

Its origins go back to Vilfredo Pareto, an economist who observed that 80% of Italy's land was owned by 20% of the population. Although it may sound vague, the 80/20 mindset can provide an insightful and infinitely applicable analysis of one-sided systems, including user interaction strategy.

The Pareto Principle states: that for many events, approximately 80% of the effects come from 20% of the causes.

To incorporate the law, focus most of your efforts on the areas that will benefit the most users.

Parkinson's Law

Formulated by Cyril Northcote Parkinson as part of the first sentence of a humorous essay published in The Economist in 1955.

Parkinson's Law: any task will increase until all available time is consumed. Limit the time required to complete a task to what users expect.

To incorporate the law: reduce the actual duration of a task compared to the expected duration, it will improve the overall user experience.

Postel's Law

John Postel, an early Internet pioneer, formulated Postel's law (also known as the persistence principle). The law is a guiding principle for software development, particularly TCP, i.e., data transfer and networking protocols. It states that "TCP implementations should conform to the general principle of reliability: be conservative in what you do, liberal in what you accept from others".

Postel's Law states: Be liberal in what you receive and conservative in what you send. Deciphering this principle in a certain sense is similar to some of Norman's heuristics.

Therefore, consider the following:

- To be responsive, flexible, and tolerant of any actions a user may take or any data they provide.
- Anticipate almost anything in terms of input, access, and capabilities, providing a reliable and accessible interface.
- The more we can predict, the more sustainable the design will be.

178

Tesler's law

While working at Xerox PARC in the mid-1980s, Larry Tesler realized that how users interact with the software is as essential as the software itself. Dan Saffer's book Designing for Interaction includes an interview with Larry Tesler describing the law of conservation of complexity. Interviews are popular among user interaction designers.

Tesler's Law, also known as the **Law of Conservation of Complexity**, states that: for any system, there is a certain amount of complexity that cannot be reduced.

To incorporate the law:

- Make sure you take as much of the burden off users as possible by dealing with internal complexity during design and development.
- Be careful not to simplify interfaces to the point of abstraction.

The von Restorff effect

The German psychiatrist and pediatrician Hedwig von Restorff (1906–1962) found in her 1933 study that if participants were presented with a list of categorically similar items with one distinctive, isolated object on the list, memory for the object would be enhanced.

The von Restorff effect, also known as the isolation effect, suggests that the one that is different from the rest is the most likely to be remembered when several similar objects are present.

To use it:

- Make important information or key actions visually prominent.

- Be careful when emphasizing visual elements to avoid competing with each other and ensure that prominent elements are not mistaken for emphasis or a state of focus.
- Don't exclude those with color vision deficiency or low vision by relying solely on color to convey contrast.
- Carefully consider motion-sensitive users when using motion to convey contrast.

Module 9: Basic UI in UX

Topic 9.1: Color theory

A study by Colorcom found that people only need 90 seconds to make a subconscious judgment about a product, and 62% to 90% of that judgment is based on color alone.

Color is a visual perception property arising from the light spectrum that interacts with the eye's photoreceptor cells.

When classifying colors, we divide them into three groups:

- Primary (red, blue, yellow).
- Secondary (mixtures of primary colors).
- Tertiary (or intermediate — mixtures of primary and secondary colors).

Color characteristics by properties:

- Hue - what it looks like (e.g. "is green").
- Chroma - how pure it is: that is, whether it has a shadow (added black), tints (added white), or tones (added gray).
- Lighting - how pale or saturated it is.

The color wheel helps you understand how different colors relate to each other and how they can be combined. There are several typical variations of color combinations that define pairs or groups of colors that go well together:

- Monochromatic: Take one shade and create other elements from its different shades and tones.
- Analog: Use three colors next to each other on the color wheel.
- Complementary: Use pairs of "opposite colors" to maximize contrast.

- Split is complementary: Add colors on either side of your complementary color pair to soften the contrast.
- Triad: Take three equally distant colours on the color wheel (i.e., 120° apart).
- Rectangular or Tetrad: Take the four colors that are two sets of complementary pairs and choose one dominant color.
- Square: 4 colors evenly spaced on the color wheel (i.e., at 90° from each other).

Color models

1) The additive model **RGB** (red, green, blue) is a mixture of the primary colors red, green, and blue. The base model for displaying colors on the screen.
2) The **CMYK** (cyan, magenta, yellow, black) subtractive model is a mixture of cyan, magenta, yellow, and black. The basic model for displaying colors when printing.
3) **HEX** is a color in hexadecimal from a grid and six values. Best for web pages.
4) **HSL** (Hue, Saturation, Lightness) - used for web pages and consists of 3 values: hue, saturation, and lightness.

It is believed that each color has its meaning and, accordingly, the style or mood it conveys. This is often taken into account in the design. However, you don't have to use colors precisely because of their meaning. Composition and matching the tone color mood of your product and brand is much more critical.

How to choose a good color combination?

- Samples and comparisons: choose several primary colors, spread them on the palette, and compare the shades.
- Combinations from the color wheel or by color value.
- Programs that generate color combinations for inspiration.

Topic 9.2: Typography

Typography is the art of arranging letters and text to make the content legible, clear, and visually appealing to the reader.

A font is a set of small and large characters, punctuation marks, numbers, and special characters of the same size and thickness for an individual typeface.

A typeface is a "set" of fonts with standard stylistic features and principles of sign construction.

Tracking is an even change in the spacing between characters throughout a block of text.

Kerning - adjusting the distance between a separate pair of characters.

The height X is the distance from the base of the letters to the top, determined by the letter x (x).

Spacing is the distance between the baselines of adjacent lines in the text.

Line spacing is the distance from the baseline to the top of the lowercase letters on the following line.

In design, we use a typographic scale in almost all projects. The title is the most important line of text that briefly describes the information in the following paragraphs and prompts you to read further exactly the paragraph where the required data is located. Typography headings are divided into levels (h1, h2, h3...).

To highlight the title on the background of other text, you must:
- Increase the distance between the heading and the paragraph.
- Increase the font size.
- Increase saturation.

Alignment is fixing the test along one of the axes. The text can be oriented differently inside the blocks depending on the task.

The main types of alignment:
- On the left edge (align left) is appropriate in 99%, consistently a winning and universal alignment option.
- In the center (align center) - for titles, short theses, quotes, and reviews, is not used in large blocks of text, is used only for accent elements, or when there are only 1-2 lines of text.
- Full (justify) - large spaces between words are formed in blocks of text with this alignment, often used for printed materials but almost never for digital products.
- On the right edge (align right) - almost not used in countries that read the text from left to right; they often align numbers this way, especially if it concerns tables.

Row width - the number of characters per line should be 40-70 characters for computers and tablets and 30-40 for phones. At the same time, the optimal pin for texts on the site is 16–20 px.

When building a project's UI, working with typography and the correct harmony of fonts is one of the main tasks. By understanding its features, you can take into account the principles of UX, manage the user's attention and correctly present the context.

Topic 9.3: Grids

Proper planning enhances the appearance of an individual object and the objects as a whole design to create a strong composition. The success of a layout depends on the placement of individual visual elements and the relationships - or visual hierarchy - formed between them. The mesh anatomy consists of several parts. Not every part is present in every grid; it depends on its type.

The format is the entire area where the final design will be placed. In print design, the format is the page, and in web design, the format is the browser window.

Margins are empty spaces between the edges of the format and the content.

Flow lines are horizontal lines that divide different areas of the grid into parallel strips. They help the reader follow the content of the layout. Flow lines also create breakpoints or edges to place elements. Some flow lines are called hanging lines, i.e., flexible, while others are called baselines.

Columns are vertical spatial zones or areas that fit from top to bottom.

Rows are horizontal spatial areas that fit entirely from left to right margin.

Gutters are spaces between rows and columns. They should always be equal between columns or rows to maintain visual balance.

When choosing a grid, pay attention to its multiplicity: the better it is thought out, the easier it is to use. Grids in multiples of 4 or 8 pixels are currently the most popular. Multiplicity defines the minor step that must be taken between different stages of the transition.

Layout grids for design projects range from one page to hundreds of pages. These are grids that organize the elements inside the space. Layout grids help designers arrange text and images in a way that looks cohesive and easy to follow.

All layout grids can be designed in two ways:

1) Symmetric grids follow the center line. Vertical fields are equal to each other, as well as horizontal. Columns in a symmetrical layout also have the same width.

2) In an asymmetric layout, both fields and columns can differ. When using an asymmetrical layout, it is essential always to find balance.

A specific grid is selected for each project:

- **Printing grids** are used in text-heavy documents, e-books, PDFs, and presentations.

- **Column grids** are used in magazines to organize content in columns to make it easier to read.

- **Basic grids** are more technical and are defined by the line in which the text is located. This grid creates a good reading rhythm for any design with lots of text.

- **Modular grids** are like a chessboard that can display many things for easy access, often used in aggregators and e-commerce products.

- **Hierarchical grids** are mainly used on websites to organize content according to its importance.

Before starting work on a new project, I recommend researching all factors, choosing classic grids that scale well, and remembering the principles of visual hierarchy and Gestalt psychology in design.

If you need to create something non-standard and asymmetric, weigh the pros and cons, consider precisely how you will present the information, how much text you use, and whether such a grid has dynamics, that is, whether this asymmetry can technically be applied to different pages.

Proper planning enhances the appearance of an individual object and the objects as a whole design to create a strong composition.

Defining the grid that will be used for the product helps us predict the page's appearance and formatting, roughly determine the amount of content, and sometimes even convey the mood of the product.

Topic 9.4: Visual Hierarchy

Visual hierarchy is the principle of arrangement of elements that allows you to show their order of importance. Designers structure visual features, such as menu icons, so users can easily understand information. Designers influence users' perceptions when placing elements logically and strategically and direct them to the desired actions. Visual hierarchy is the principle of managing the user's attention.

The visual hierarchy on the product page is built from the following:

- Size – users notice larger elements more easily.
- Color – bright colors usually attract more attention than muted ones.
- Contrast - sharply contrasting colors attract attention.
- Alignment - elements that are not aligned are highlighted above those that are aligned.
- Repetition – repeating styles can indicate related content.
- Proximity - it is determined that closely spaced elements seem related.
- Whitespace - more space around elements draws attention to them.
- Texture and style - richer textures stand out over flat ones.

The following elements of visual hierarchy can be added to the classic distribution by size: text weight, stylistic applications, and even a hierarchy of indents. By correctly forming the hierarchy of the text, we help the user to scan it faster and therefore spend less time searching for important information.

Color. Color allows you to direct the user and focus his attention on the elements that are most important to us. Therefore, for example, CTA call-to-action buttons are usually made in bright or very contrasting colors. Color can be manipulated both with the help of contrasts and with the help of shades of the same color.

Contrast helps determine what you want the viewer to look at first. Contrast draws the eye to a particular area. Technically, this is a visible difference in the properties of structural elements. Any difference can be defined as contrast, but for graphic design, which is often used for marketing purposes, it should be significant enough to distinguish one from the other clearly.

Closeness or relatedness: the human brain groups together elements that are similar, sorted, or have common characteristics.

Texture and style are other methods of building hierarchy often used in design and marketing to draw attention. An essential CTA should stand out and be visually more interesting than others to attract attention.

Reading patterns were determined based on text scanning and visual context hierarchy. They explain how users "process" certain information and help designers place components on accent lines to increase the focal point and make the user look precisely at a specific piece.

- Z-Pattern is primarily intended for pages with minimal copy.
- F-Pattern - It is believed that in the absence of subheadings and bullets, users tend to focus on words at the beginning of lines and the top of the page.

Gestalt principles are principles/laws of human perception that describe how humans group similar elements, recognize patterns, and simplify complex images when we perceive objects:

- Invariance
- Similarity
- Closing
- Grouping (proximity)
- The law of the figure
- General fate (movement)

There is another way to add hierarchy to content. Namely - its absence - or what we call white or negative space. This is the space around the content and functional elements of the page. The primary role of white space is to allow your design to breathe by reducing the amount of text and functionality users see at once.

Topic 9.5: Composition

Composition is a concept that defines a combination of different elements that come together and form a common understanding or product. Literally, composition means the placement or arrangement of visual elements on a blank page, but in the design sense, we refer to composition as the art of combining elements.

Composition is one of the fundamental principles of graphic design. Understanding it will help you achieve attractive, expressive, and coherent works when studying visual elements. Colors, shape, space, and symmetry are just a few aspects to consider in a creative composition.

The composition is managed by:

- Dimensions
- Visual hierarchy
- White space

- Balance of elements
- Complementarity
- Contrasts
- Placement of objects

and other.

By definition, using the composition as a methodology allows you to combine different aspects of specific elements to create a whole.

The rule of thirds

It can be applied to any subject to improve the composition and balance of your images. This is one of the most useful composition techniques, acting as a guide to help creators to determine where to place an object or resource.

This theory is a simple, effective method of dividing your canvas/artboard into thirds horizontally/vertically, resulting in 4 intersection points. These are ideal places to place focal points in your design (the top left is where your viewers are looking the most).

Using the rule of thirds will allow you to position design elements correctly so that the overall composition conveys the right message, is well-balanced, easy to understand, and looks fantastic!

Golden ratio

The golden ratio is a standard mathematical ratio found in nature to create natural-looking compositions in your design work. Sometimes it is called divine proportions. A series of interlocking golden rectangles form a golden spiral shape. Using these proportions creates a more attractive picture and allows us to direct the user's attention to the element that is most interesting to us.

Guide users

Just as you point to something when you want people to look at it, by placing certain lines and shapes in a certain way, you can control the point of view of your design, meaning where the viewer's eyes look when they see your design.

An everyday use of leader lines that you may be familiar with is flowcharts. Flowcharts use lines to guide your gaze from one point to another in an obvious way.

Contrasts

Use contrasts to draw users' attention to essential elements. Contrast is a handy tool for highlighting and hiding certain design elements. Increasing the contrast or using a high-contrast color can help an element stand out and draw attention. Likewise, by reducing the contrast, you can make an element disappear into the background.

Contrast is not only color. It can be shape, size, placement, technology, or orientation.

Alignment, proportions

When creating a composition with many elements, don't just put them all on the page and forget about them because aligning them is a quick and easy way to take your design from shabby to chic. The easiest way to understand composition is in terms of alignment through proportions and focal elements.

The composition is unique for each product and depends a lot on the product usage and attributes. Typically composition is divided into static and dynamic.

- **Static.** It is saved regardless of changes to the page. An example is the Google search window; the entire composition remains static while you are on the same page.
- **Dynamic.** Adapts to requests and changes. Examples are sites of aggregators and online stores; for example, the site booking.com changes dynamically according to the filters, search, or sorting that the user can configure on the site.

Topic 9.6: Spacing and Shadows

Spacing is the distance between elements in the UI, which is added to divide content into groups or structuring components. It helps to organize information and sets your design's rhythm, structure, and hierarchy. These factors work together to help the designer to have a rational approach to elements such as spacing.

The correct spacing:

- Helps me to understand the hierarchy and grouping of elements on the page.
- Developers can place elements on a page without the involvement of a designer.
- Designers can place elements on a page in less than 30 seconds.

Base units help to determine the step to which the elements in the system will correspond. We have already mentioned this in the topic of the layout grid. However, base units are a somewhat more general concept; we can use them not only for the grid but also for any other elements as a step for the typographic scale, icons, and other graphics. Using such step values can be used by the designer to maintain a consistent product and reduce the time the designer spends communicating and changing the design.

A shadow is a dark area where an opaque object blocks light from a light source. It occupies the entire three-dimensional volume behind the thing with the light in front. A cross-section of a shadow is a two-dimensional silhouette or a reverse projection of an object blocking the light.

The use of shadows in design is based on the rules of physics since, in the real world, everything is dimensional, and elements interact with each other in three-dimensional space: they can be stacked or attached to each other but cannot pass through each other. Objects also cast shadows and reflect light. Understanding these interactions is fundamental to our understanding of the GUI.

With the help of elevation, we can separate objects. The elevation is the measured value from the front of one surface to another; the height of an element indicates the distance between surfaces and the depth of its shadow. As you can see in the image, the shadow becomes more significant and more blurred the further the distance between the object and the ground.

To visualize shadows, use:

- Blur (blurry effect) can organically fit into the website's design.
- Shadow components to define a shadow that can be adjusted according to space parameters.
- Shift (offset) or shift elements along the axes; depending on the height of your light source, the shift can increase or decrease.
- Color, typically objects that are closer to us appear brighter to us.

The main mistakes of working with shadows

1) Shadows are too bulky and heavy for the components, primarily for beginners who don't yet know how to set up the right combinations of color and dispersion. This creates a rather strange and unaesthetic effect and does not correspond to the basic principle because we get dark spots, not highlights and shadows.

2) You are using multi-colored shadows in different directions. This error usually occurs due to inattention. Sometimes you can do this, but you need to understand that it serves as a focal element and will draw attention to the component. Therefore, do not make all the shadows different, which applies not only to the direction but also to the sizes or colors.

3) Using unnatural shadows that break the hierarchy. This mistake is often found when designers do not understand or do not take into account the physical nature of the shadow and place it not in accordance with the hierarchy but on the eye.

Topic 9.7: Basics of iconography

An icon is a schematic or detailed image used to indicate specific details in the interface. Icons are often used as an allegory or association. This is not new; hieroglyphs and similar drawings to represent concepts and words have been used long before digitization.

Why are they used?

- Icons are easy to recognize. If you use familiar icons in your designs, your audience will instantly remember them, helping with navigation and tasks.

- They save space. This advantage is significant on mobile phones, where icons can save valuable space.

195

- The icons are an excellent focus-area to touch. The recommended icon size for mobile devices is 1 cm by 1 cm, which is about 44 x 44 px, ideal for finger tapping.
- They are universal. The meaning of such icons can be easily understood even if users do not speak your language.
- They are aesthetically attractive. If icons are well-designed, they can make a website or app more visually appealing.

Classification of icons

Colored. They can have a solid color or a gradient color scheme, making icons less formal and more playful. The disadvantage of colored icons is that they are more challenging to integrate into the product's aesthetics and can even distract users from meaningful content. Because of this, overuse tends to hurt UX.

Two-colored. Icons contain two similar colors that are clearly separated. To create one, you take an icon, split its elements into two layers (such as an outline and a fill), choose a starting shade, experiment with the layer's opacity, and a two-color icon is born.

Outlined. Vector strokes create them, and inside they are empty. They have pros and cons. On the other hand, they are clean, minimalist, and can look very sophisticated. On the other hand, users may take longer to process and recognize.

Universals. This group is immediately recognizable and usually represents repetitive actions such as the home page, print, or search. Universal icons should represent universal actions in your product to make sure everything is clear.

When creating icons, remember about:

- Grids. Using grids, you'll spend less time ensuring all your icons work together and make fewer mistakes.
- Spacing. These should be adjusted for each icon to ensure they are visually consistent.
- Roundness or corner radius (the number of corners that are pointed or rounded) is another key to creating visually consistent icons. If one icon has sharp corners, you should also ensure that all other icons have sharp corners.

Topic 9.8: Responsive and Adaptive design

A website with a responsive design looks almost the same on all devices, but this site is fluid and changes its layout and appearance depending on the size and orientation of the device. For this, flexible grids and layouts are widely used, and it is planned how this or that layout will look at different screen sizes and proportions.

In adaptive design, a separate website layout is created for each device screen. When loading, the site recognizes the screen size and displays the layout created for that viewport. In fact, you can create a different user experience for each of the six standard screen sizes from very small to very large: 320px, 480px, 760px, 960px, 1200px, and 1600px.

However, since developing a website for six different screen sizes would be incredibly time-consuming, the work can be limited to referring to user analytics for the existing version of the site to determine the screen sizes on which users often access it.

Responsive - best used for new products, requires significantly less work to build and maintain, allows you to create a unified experience for all users, and distinguishes between features available for desktop and mobile devices, requiring more code and configuration.

Adaptive - better used to improve existing products, adapts better to "specific" screen sizes, allows the designer to provide a unique experience for each screen size or use case, and loads faster. Still, the site might not be formatted for non-standard sizes.

Mobile First Principle - mobile design is a key component of successful product design. Designing for the smallest screens first and improving later allows designers to focus on the core features of their product. When you focus on the essence of your product and discard the rest, you can pinpoint the essential UX components. Then, when you start designing for larger screens, you can add additional elements to complement the product's or service's core features.

Five principles of Mobile first design:

1) Users are the drivers of design: Your design should help users solve a problem or complete a task quickly and efficiently.

2) Visual Content Hierarchy: Your content should be concise and to the point. It's essential to focus on delivering only what the user is looking for while cutting out the details that might distract them.

3) Make it simpler: A simple mobile design is a great way to improve content clarity, helping users focus on the most critical content.

4) Prominent and consistent CTAs: Bright, bold, and consistent CTAs help users quickly find them.

5) Pay attention to your site's loading speed: For example, if users experience poor website performance, 79% of buyers are less likely to purchase from that website again.

Topic 9.9: Mobile UX

Mobile UX design is user experience design for portable devices.

The difference between a good app and a bad one is usually the quality of its user interface (UX). Today's mobile users expect a lot from an app: fast loading, ease of use, and fun interaction. If you want your app to be successful, you need to consider UX not just a secondary aspect of design but an essential component of your product strategy.

Some tips for a successful mobile:

- Keep content to a minimum (give the user only what they need to know).
- Minimize interface elements. The simple design will provide the user with convenience in using the product.
- Use the progressive reveal technique to show more options and not overload the interface.
- Break tasks into small pieces, forms into steps, and tables into separate active areas.
- Customize the keyboard according to the request type. Show a numeric keypad when asking for a phone number, and add an @ button for an email address.
- Identify the steps in the user journey where users may need assistance.

Maintaining an overall consistent look and feel throughout the application is important. As far as the mobile app is concerned, sequence means the following:

- Visual consistency
- Functional consistency
- External consistency

The most crucial element on the screen should have the most visual weight. Adding more weight to an element is possible with font thickness, size, and color.

Remember the touch zones.

The design of mobile applications can be created custom, from their components, and native, according to guidelines. In native design, we expect the layouts and product to conform as closely as possible to the principles, rules, and guidelines of the platform we're building the product for. Custom applications assume that they can be unified for all platforms and use unique components that may be uncharacteristic for a particular platform.

The guidelines for each platform describe in detail all their application components, elements, and rules. Typically, these guidelines are created as a system design that can be reused. Guides are not static; they are updated frequently, keep your finger on the pulse.

Material design

In 2014, Google introduced its Material Design guidelines as a design language focused on creating a great user experience on a growing number of connected devices. The concept aims to provide flexible principles to create an adaptive interface. The Material Design specification contains guidelines for everything: typography, grids, space, scale, color, and images. But Material Design goes beyond just telling designers how to make a product look cool; it's about functionality and interactions.

Material design is more like a set of components; the guide describes the interaction, patterns, rules of use, features of the dimensional grid, rules of combination, and more.

Human Interface Design

These are software development documents that offer software developers a set of guidelines. They aim to improve the user experience by making application interfaces more intuitive, learnable, and consistent. For this, both methodical information and specific examples are provided. Human Interface Design contains various recommendations and requirements for creating products for various Apple platforms. Some of the components used are specific to this platform.

Some tips for learning how to work with mobile design

- Understand the terminology.
- Understand the dimensions and behavior of components for different screen types.
- Practice working with components and guides.
- Learn about mobile-specific rules and guidelines.

Topic 9.10: Atomic Design

Atomic Design is a methodology created by Brad Frost that seeks to provide guidelines for designing interface design systems more thoughtfully and with clear order and hierarchy. This methodology is called atomic design because the idea is based on chemistry and the study of the composition of matter.

The universe is made up of a fixed set of "atomic elements" known to many of us as the periodic table of elements. These elements are the building blocks of everything that surrounds us.

There are five distinct steps in the atomic design methodology, with the first three modeled after their equivalents in the world of chemistry:

- Atoms
- Molecules
- Organisms
- Templates
- Pages

Each subsequent stage builds on the previous one, collecting elements from previous stages.

As in chemistry, **atoms** are the smallest building blocks in our system. Instead of atoms like Oxygen or Hydrogen, in the design, we have buttons, inputs, colors, fonts, labels, and other small elements used in it. An example would be icons, as they are small elements that combine to form the next step, molecules.

At the molecule stage, we take our independent atomic design elements, each with their characteristics, style, and format, and combine them into new groups. As in chemistry, molecules can consist of 2 or more atoms; one atom can be used in many molecules.

As we progress to the stage of **organisms**, our collections of atoms and molecules become more complex than at the molecular level. Atoms and molecules, such as text, color, icons, buttons, etc., are certainly necessary. Still, objects are more "alienated" and self-contained at the level of molecules. In contrast, when molecules are transformed into an organism, they can have a context, perform functions, and have variations. Organisms can consist of similar and/or different types of molecules.

The pattern is the first step of the Atomic Design methodology, which does not correspond to the steps in the molecular world but is essential to the

Atomic Design principle. A template is where we assemble our organisms and other elements into a single design.

Pages are the final step in the Atomic Design methodology. In the design process, you may not design pages for each instance. Still, it is helpful to create several options when your data changes; different profile information or languages may affect the design of your template. Page-level development allows you to test these variations and adapt your templates globally.

The atomic design provides a straightforward methodology for creating design systems. Clients and team members can better appreciate the concept of design systems by seeing the steps in front of them.

Topic 9.11: Design System

A design system is a set of reusable components governed by transparent standards that can be put together to create any number of applications. The design of the system usually includes:

- Style guide
- Components (synchronized with FE)
- Documentation

A design system is not just a set of assets and components you use to create a digital product. When is a design system needed? To get started, ask the team the following questions:

1) Does prototyping take you much time? Is your product complex, with complex components and scenarios?

2) Do you create the same things over and over again? Reuse components and fragments of designs?

3) Do you create one or more products?

If you answered "yes" at least once, the design system is for you. But before starting to work on it, igniting the team and the customer, ask designers and developers one more question:

4) Can you make sure that everyone will use and maintain the system?

- How to create a design system?
- Conduct a visual audit.
- Create a visual design language.
- Create a library of interface components/templates.

5) Document. Documentation and standards separate a template library from a proper design system.

Interesting design systems that everyone should know about:

- Atlassian
- Carbon
- Material
- Nachos
- Polaris

When the design system is NOT needed:

1) When you work on a single, small project, and maybe even are the only designer.

2) If you or your client is not ready to spend resources on creating and maintaining a system design.

3) If you develop modules or products for other organizations as an organization.

Design systems can quickly and thoroughly transfer knowledge without relying on specific people. Many products and companies require them but consider your specific conditions and needs before starting anything.

Topic 9.12: Accessibility

Accessibility in the basic theory of design is understood as a convenience that is the same for everyone. Accessibility describes methodologies for creating products that are understandable and accessible to people of all backgrounds and abilities. Inclusive design can address accessibility, age, culture, economic status, education, gender, geographic location, language, and race. The focus is on meeting the needs of as many users as possible, not just the majority.

We take into account the following:
- Color
- Type
- Sound
- The image is different

The improvement process focuses on ensuring that interfaces and technologies can be used by people with disabilities (including hearing, cognitive, physical, and visual disabilities). Accessibility is narrower in scope than inclusive design because it focuses on specific accommodations.

Additionally, accessibility standards such as the Web Content Accessibility Guidelines (WCAG) make it easier to evaluate accessibility versus inclusive and universal design. However, accessibility is only the minimum for a meaningful experience for people with disabilities.

Availability for whom? To all. In almost every case you can think of, your product needs to function. For example, in different environments or depending on the situation, when you are calm and have no time limit, and when you are in a hurry. Or depending on physical capabilities, when a person can use two hands or only one.

Some patterns that help "blur the boundaries" and make products comfortable for everyone take into account the interests or characteristics of everyone, not just the majority:

- Diversity of demographic identifiers.
- Various illustrations.
- Colors.
- Visual focus indication for keyboard focus.
- Forms.
- Text legibility and dark mode for older users.
- Hover and others.

Accessibility rules are NOT:

- A barrier to innovation
- Unification

Accessibility isn't about anyone, in particular, it's about everyone, and designers who adhere to these principles create a level playing field for everyone, regardless of background, ability, background, or capability.

You can read more about accessibility in the following documents:

1) WCAG 2.1 - guidelines for accessibility of web content.

2) EN 301549 - regulation of accessibility of ICT products and services in the EU, covers all types of basic technologies from tablets or e-book readers to ATMs.

3) Instructions for individual devices (such as telephones or washing machines) that remain relevant if such devices are digitally enhanced.

4) European Accessibility Act - which aims to remove barriers created by different accessibility regulations in different countries.

When starting development, keep accessibility requirements in mind to ensure a better customer experience; sooner or later, you will have to take care of it.

Topic 9.13: Mood boards and visual research

A Mood board is a visual tool that communicates our concepts and visual ideas. It is a well-thought-out and planned arrangement of images, materials, pieces of text, etc., intended to plan or project a particular style or concept.

They are used to:

- Structure the process of building a clear design story that we want to use in the space.
- Express the vision of the project that you have in mind.

This is a good starting point for achieving results and validating visual solutions. Creating a mood board is a relatively simple method, but even it can be misused.

- To begin with, do not limit yourself to design solutions; rely only on style ideas.
- Don't copy ideas, be inspired by them.
- Do not "steal" designs; find patterns in them, study them.
- Get inspired by the mood board, and then "hide" it. Don't start designing and follow the mood board too closely.

How to create a mood board

1) When creating a mood board, try not to pay attention to identical designs or competitors' options.

2) Decide on the topic, and what it is in general.

- How would you like to see the product?
- What does he look like?

- Color? Texture? Template? Emotion or feeling?

3) Create a mood board using Figma, a Pinterest board, or upload images you like (and convey the desired emotion).

4) Identify the main elements of similarity in the images you have chosen.

Initially, the mood boards created were physical; even now, you can still find physical mood boards in fashion design and sometimes interior design. They include visual and tactile elements, such as different materials, textures, or other types. Therefore, you need to think of a mood board not only as a set of images.

Visual research methods (VRM) include visual elements such as maps, drawings, photographs, videos, and 3D objects added to the research process to test and gather user information.

As with any UX research, recruit test participants representative of your target audience. They don't need to have a background in design - people don't need a background in visual design to know if they like something; in fact, users can reliably rate how much they like the visual.

As we conduct research, we can test our assumptions about style or components by:

- Interview
- Polls and surveys
- Testing concepts, grids, compositions, etc.

Several options for visual tests

- **5-second Test:** In this, you show a stimulus (image, prototype, mood board, etc.) for 5 seconds (or another short period of time). This approach is best for accurately capturing people's "gut reactions." 5 seconds of viewing is not enough to read the content or notice details like certain fonts or colors. Still, it is enough to form an impression that accurately reflects the visual style.

- **First Click Test**: you give participants specific instructions (e.g., "Learn more about this organization") before they are introduced to the design and stop them after they click on a place on the screen where they can complete the task.

- **Comparison of several design options:** often showing users several possible visual designs helps them to determine what they like (or don't like) about each option. If you ask participants to rate more than one design, be sure to change the order in which they see the alternatives, as some of the people's responses may depend on which version they see first.

How to evaluate user feedback

It can be estimated using the following approaches:

1) Open-ended explanation of benefits: Ask users why they like the design.

2) Open word choice: Ask users to list 3 to 5 words that describe the design.

3) Closed word choice (desirability test): Give users a list of terms and ask them to choose the words that best describe the design.

4) Numerical scores: collect numerical scores on how well the design demonstrates certain brand qualities (e.g., on a scale of 1 to 5).

Module 10: Prototyping and testing

Topic 10.1: Wireframing

A wireframe is a two-dimensional illustration of a page's interface that focuses explicitly on allocating space and prioritizing content, available features, and intended behavior.

Wireframes help:

- Connect the information architecture of the site with its visual design, showing paths between pages.
- Explain consistent ways to display certain types of information in a user interface.
- Determine the intended functionality of the interface.
- Prioritize content by determining how much space to allocate for a given element and where that element is located.

Typically, wireframes should be as fast as possible in creation; this is their main functionality and purpose. If you understand that wireframes take too much time and the detailing has become too detailed - they need to be simplified.

The wireframing process typically occurs during the prototyping phase of a product. At this stage, designers test the scope of the product, collaborate on ideas, and work out the flow details. A wireframe is usually an initial iteration of a product used as a design's starting point. But this is not the only option. Wireframes can actually be used in almost any phase, for example, in the

211

discovery phase if we are working with an existing product or in the research phase when we are looking at specific ideas or wire flows. This is usually an intermediate stage. And armed with valuable insights from initial user feedback, designers can create the next, more detailed iteration of a product design, such as a full-scale prototype or mockup.

There are three typical types of wireframes:

Low fidelity. Non-detailed drawings and sketches that help facilitate project team communication and develop relatively quickly. They tend to be more abstract because they often use simple images to block space and use mockup content, or Latin (lorem ipsum) text as placeholders for content and labels, i.e., placeholders

Advantage: Speed.

High-fidelity. Detailed wireframes are better for documenting because of their increased level of detail. These images often contain information about each specific element on the page, including the dimensions, behavior, and/or actions associated with any interactive element. It can still be black and white but detailed.

Advantage: Accuracy.

Mid-fidelity. Less quick but more detailed option, mainly used for testing and presentations.

Advantage: higher quality but still low cost.

The detail and elements we include in the wire largely depend on low, medium, or high accuracy; there is no clear list of what exactly should be there. They are traditionally created in shades of gray, so designers often play with shading - using lighter shades of gray to represent lighter colors and darker shades to represent brighter colors. You can sometimes add color in high-precision wires, such as red to indicate a warning or error message or dark blue to indicate an active link.

Wireframes are fast. This is an outline for the project to help you and your team think through and agree on a structure. The wireframes make it clear that this is not the final design. No one could confuse the wire with the final appearance of your application. Low fidelity and color limitations force you to focus on structure rather than detail. There will be plenty of time for visual design once the framework is complete.

Should you use wireframes?

Yes, if:
- Your job is to visualize and iterate quickly.
- The product is complex and requires a lot of planning, research, and validation.
- This is embedded in the design process for the team and approval by stakeholders.

No, if:
- You use a detailed design system.
- The task or product is straightforward, trivial, and typical.
- If other rapid prototyping alternatives are used.

Topic 10.2: Prototyping

Prototyping is a process in which teams of designers generate ideas, experiment with them, and bring concepts to life, from ideas on paper to digital design.

At its core, a prototype is an early sample of a product that allows users to visualize or interact with it before the final product is developed. This is the fourth step of the design thinking process, followed by usability testing.

A prototype without further testing is wasted time.

Objectives of prototyping:

1) Learning new ideas. Prototypes allow designers to experiment with different ideas and solutions. They give the developer the freedom to test multiple potential scenarios while tweaking them to optimize the usability of the final product.

2) Identification of problems. Prototypes are a great way to gain a deeper understanding of the problem a user is facing. They enable designers to better understand a product or system by interacting with it and seeing what works and doesn't.

3) To detect usability problems. User interaction prototyping is a great way to uncover usability issues with your product.

Types of prototypes

Low-fidelity or low-fi prototypes, often called paper prototypes, are the fastest, least-effort prototypes that can be created.

They represent a simple, incomplete version of your product and are a great way to test high-level concepts before investing more time and energy into design.

Low-fidelity prototypes also allow you to gather feedback and test concepts early in the design process. Because they are created with pen and paper, designers can quickly test different concepts, allowing them to be adjusted accordingly before moving on to digital wireframes.

Medium-fidelity prototypes are the next level of prototyping. Medium-fidelity prototypes, often called wireframes, are digital and created in shades of gray. They limit the design to user flows and information architecture, omitting branding elements, photos, and logos. In other words, it's like a high-fidelity wireframe prototype, we still don't care about the perfect final look, but now the connections and specific components are critical.

Limiting the prototype to user flows and information architecture in grayscale allows the user to focus on the fundamental aspects of the design without being distracted by colors, photo placement, and logos. This allows the designer to test the product's usability before decorating it.

High-fidelity prototype. After several rounds of testing with low- and medium-fidelity prototypes, it's time to spend time rendering your design in high fidelity. That's when the designer uses branding, photography, copy, color, and animation to bring the experience to life. As your development nears its final stages, testing high-fidelity prototypes with users before the development stage is essential.

How to create a prototype

1) Select the key features you want to test on users. It is impossible to effectively test all the features of your product in one session.
2) Next, create a prototype of your website or app to demonstrate the key features and flows identified in the previous step.
3) Present your design to users, partners, and stakeholders. Observe and record their interactions with your product, noting any usability issues in the current design.
4) Iteratively test and update the prototype. After the testing session, synthesize your feedback into critical takeaways and edit your designs accordingly.

Typical mistakes

1) Creating a prototype without a clear goal often happens when you are already too enthusiastic about the process and want to see the final product. Still, you need to distinguish between mockups and prototypes.

2) Prototyping too early, initial prototypes are usually not saved; they will still have many changes.

3) Using the wrong prototyping tool (bye-bye PowerPoint). And so this is a real case.

4) Using placeholder text and images instead of actual data might be fine for wireframes or low- to mid-level prototypes, but if we're doing detailed prototypes, it makes them a lot worse.

5) Feedback late in the process is wrong - prototypes are iterative, and if they don't iterate with feedback and improvement, it diminishes their value.

6) And the most typical mistake of beginners is to get too attached to the prototype. You can especially not comment here, but this is a real case, and sometimes you learn to "not get attached" only with experience. You should always be prepared that a particular piece of work may be unsuccessful and will be discarded, but this is not bad; we want to make mistakes because, at the design stage, our mistakes are still not too expensive.

Topic 10.3: Guerilla testing

Guerilla testing (also known as corridor usability testing) is a relatively quick and informal way to test ideas, get high-level feedback, and identify potential user interaction issues. Such testing can be done almost anywhere: in a coffee shop, a shopping center, in an office corridor or on the street. Ideally, you'll test 8-10 users in a hallway test, each typically lasting about 10 minutes.

Advantages of corridor testing:
- It's that you can move quickly.
- If you don't have the budget for research, it's better than no testing.
- It is incredibly cheap compared to more formal studies.

How to conduct guerrilla testing

1) Define a goal. Why do you do this? Set a reasonable goal, remembering that this is only a 10-minute test. For example, if you have a complex flow of 20 steps, try to analyze whether it is possible to divide it into fragments that will be smaller but will not lose their logical connection.

2) Come up with a pitch. A short proposal with an explanation of up to 20-30 seconds why strangers should participate in your testing. Briefly explain precisely what you are doing and what will happen. The pitch will not always be successful; many people will immediately refuse, even before you explain the point; this is normal, but try to make it as open as possible, without the unnecessary jargon and professional vocabulary.

3) Give preference to diversity when choosing participants. Move around. You need short tests with different participants, not repeated sessions with a single target group.

4) Be clear about what you need from the participant. If you want them to look at a prototype, talk out loud, and tell you if they can figure something out - articulate that.

5) Make a note of the feedback. Unlike classic testing, this type does not rely on audio or video recording, firstly, it will be challenging to organize, as many will not want to permit you, and also, these results will be more challenging to analyze because the test scenario itself will be less structured, which means there will be more correlation and chatter.

When you finish the test, you will have a lot of notes and memos. Organize them by participants, and don't mix them up. Write your conclusions, quotes, or guesses on stickers. Place them on the table, on the wall, or in another place that will allow you to "look at the results from the side."

Now that you have a bunch of stickers for each scenario group them by the themes you find. The big themes are the ones that came from the most participants. Smaller topics are those that came from fewer people. You can use thematization techniques, such as affinity mapping, to systematize them. How to group - choose yourself; it can be by similarity, by a standard topic or mood, related to a specific question, or conversely, by the type of answer from the participant. You can make small explanations for the groups or summarize them. Figuring out the "why" of the problem may require further exploration of some concepts.

This testing is often used on versions that appear pretty early in the development process and is far from ideal. Although this testing is not very informative compared to other methods, its key feature is precisely its speed since planning testing sessions usually take a lot of time.

Topic 10.4: Usability testing

Usability testing is checking and validating ideas, prototypes, and other concepts. During a usability testing session, a researcher (called a "facilitator" or "moderator") asks the participant to complete a task, usually using one or more specific user interfaces and a detailed description of what or even how to do it. As the participant completes each task, the researcher observes their behavior and listens for feedback.

Usability testing goals:
- Identifying problems in the design of a product or service.
- Disclosure of improvement opportunities.
- Studying the behavior and preferences of the target user.

The usability testing method has several advantages:
- It determines whether the participants can successfully complete the specified tasks and the duration of the specified tasks.
- Identifies changes needed to improve productivity and user satisfaction.
- It provides simplicity and ease of use.

How to conduct usability testing

There are many different types of usability testing, but the essential elements of most usability tests are a facilitator, a task, and a participant.

The **facilitator** guides the participant through the testing process. Gives instructions, answers participants' questions, and asks additional questions.

The **tasks** in the usability test are realistic actions that the participant can perform in real life. They can be very specific or very open, depending on the tasks.

The **participant** must be an actual user of the product or service being studied (or a potential one with a high level of accuracy).

1) To get started, decide what part of the product or website you want to test.
2) Select a task or scenario to test.
3) Set the standard of success (success criteria, number of sessions, etc.).
4) Write a test plan and script.
5) Identify a facilitator.
6) Select participants (screening welcome).
7) Do your research.

8) Analyze your data.

When building a task scenario or defining a goal, make sure it is logical and consistent. For a user, you'll typically need to specify an Environment, a condition, and a task. That is, you must understand the general story: where will you conduct testing, what is the user's situation, what are his goals with the product, and what are the conditions. For example, most tests can be performed simply in an office or a unique laboratory. Still, there are also those for which the environment is as important as the task, so you may need to create conditions, for example, poor lighting or poor Internet, or using the product with only one hand, or others. Some situations are obvious and intersect with the life experience of users, while others require clarification and a more detailed explanation.

Usability testing is divided into several types. According to the nature of information collection, it can be quantitative or qualitative.

Qualitative usability testing focuses on gathering information, findings, and quotes about how people use a product or service. Qualitative usability testing is best suited for identifying problems in user interaction. This form of usability testing is more common than quantitative testing.

Quantitative usability testing focuses on collecting metrics that describe the user experience. The two metrics most commonly collected in quantitative usability testing are task success and task completion time. Quantitative usability testing is best for gathering benchmarks.

According to the type of facilitation, usability testing is divided into moderated and unmoderated; sometimes, they are mixed.

Remote moderated usability tests work very similarly to in-person studies. The presenter continues interacting with the participant and asks him to complete the task. However, the facilitator and participant may be in different physical locations. Typically, moderated tests can be done using screencasting software such as Skype or GoToMeeting.

Remote unmoderated usability tests do not have the same facilitator-participant interaction as in-person or moderated tests. The researcher uses a unique online remote testing tool to customize the writing tasks for the participant. Then the participant completes these tasks on his own in his free time. The test tool provides instructions for the task and any follow-up questions. After the participant completes their test, the researcher receives a session recording and metrics such as task performance.

After testing, you need to analyze it in detail. Typically you can have three types of results for a task:

1) It went well, and the user succeeded.
2) It didn't go well, but we understand why.
3) It didn't go well, but we need more research and activities to understand exactly why the problem occurred.

In the usability report, we include the following:

1) Title page.
- Your company logo (if applicable).
- The name of the company/product for which you are conducting a usability test.
- Names of researchers involved in the preparation of the report.
- Report creation date.

2) Resume or executive summary.
- List the most important results of the tests you performed.
- Include key findings, the purpose of the study, and how and where it was conducted.

- Start by mentioning how and why you tested the product.
- Use statistics to highlight key research factors, e.g., How many participants successfully completed the task?

3) Goals.

- Your report goals should be clear and concise so your team can refer back to them after testing.
- Clearly state the main goals you want to achieve when conducting user testing.

4) Methodology.

- Explain how you did the testing.
- How did you select participants?
- This can be especially important if your audience is unfamiliar with the methodology or if you're sending a report and they won't be able to ask you questions immediately; this will help to avoid misunderstandings.

5) Profile of participants.

- Add a summary, including your test group's age range and other information.
- Provide key details, including professional education, age, income, and gender, if applicable.
- Pay attention only to those factors that were decisive for you in the screening. I also don't recommend including photos or real names of members, use encoding.

6) Tasks and scenarios that were checked.

- List all the steps you asked users to take.

7) Results and recommendations.

- Here you will show stakeholders how you organized, analyzed and synthesized all the data collected during your usability testing research.
- Create different categories to group your findings.

- Include "positive" and "negative" observations and data in a paragraph or two.

Topic 10.5: A/B testing

A/B testing compares two versions (A and B) of the same web page or application to determine which one performs better. Versions are randomly displayed to different users at the same time. An A/B test doesn't have to be just two options. You can also create multiple variants, and these experiments are called A/B/N testing, where N is a certain number of options you try. The difference between versions is usually quite small; we don't want to have radically different layouts because the results will be impossible to evaluate.

You can analyze how your visitors interact with these versions by dividing the traffic between the two versions in the A/B testing process. This lets you identify the version that captures more visitor activity or conversions.

Advantages:

- The thing about A/B testing is that it allows you to make product design decisions based on data, not assumptions.
- It can improve the product's overall user experience and increase your conversion rate.
- Much more efficient approach than implementing right away, as it saves you time and resources spent on expensive pre-market testing.

Before conducting A/B testing, it is necessary not only to prepare mock-ups and make changes to the test version of the finished product but also to prepare a specific rationale. As always, we begin by defining goals. It is also essential to note exactly how we will compare the options and evaluate the results at this stage. KPIs or metrics can be typical.

KPIs will be based on the goals we set for the product. Example:
- Number of sales for a specific product line.
- Income from existing customers.
- Increasing the level of retention of current customers.
- The number of job applicants.
- Uploading an offer with high lead efficiency.
- Reaching a new audience or demographic.
- Expanding market share.
- Increasing brand awareness.
- Increasing the number of conversions to paid advertising, and many others.

Metrics, in turn, will be more specific about the indicators we measure but more generalized about the goals. Example:
- Number of form submissions.
- Number of jumps to the page.
- Number of subscriptions.
- Number of articles read.
- Transition and bounce rate.
- Number of comments.
- Percentage of purchases by shares in social networks.
- Number of jumps to product pages.

Types of A/B testings

1) Testing split URLs.

With split URL testing, you can compare different versions of the same page hosted on different URLs. Inbound traffic is split between these two versions, and the performance is tracked to determine the winner. Unlike basic A/B testing, where you experiment with tiny elements or minor interface changes, split URL testing is used when the two versions differ significantly in design or code. However, using this option also needs to be thought out. For example, apply it with too large and significant changes. It will be difficult to monitor and evaluate the results because specific changes may be better or worse but interchangeable and correlated in a more global plan. The method is suitable when you need to test specific layouts or versions that must be viewed comprehensively. For example, different color schemes. Or other formats of the registration form, etc.

2) A multivariate or multinomial test is an extension of the typical A/B test. While a standard A/B test allows you to test only one element or variable simultaneously, a multivariate test allows you to try more than one element on a web page. While basic A/B testing allows you to compare CTA button copy, multivariate testing allows you to test different combinations of headlines, subheadings, and CTAs. Analyzing the results of multivariate testing is more difficult than when using two variants; for this, a decision tree is often used. When several options are launched simultaneously, their results are compared according to the principle of pairs; for example, we start with 8, choose 4 with the highest rating, then 2, and then choose the final option.

3) Multi-page testing, also known as funnel testing, is another form of A/B testing where instead of making changes to a single page, changes are made to a sequence of pages or a specific flow. You can test elements on different pages and see the impact these changes have on the buyer journey on your website. Multi-page testing is typically used to test different types of content, design theories, or sales and support strategies.

When choosing the type of A/B testing, pay attention to the primary goal, the traffic you need to attract, and some irregularity. That is, users should receive different versions in a truly random way and not based on certain characteristics or roles.

To conduct A/B testing

1) Select one variable to test.

2) Define your goal. What do you want to achieve or test?

3) Create a "control variant" and a "contender."

4) Divide the sample groups equally and randomly.

5) Determine the sample size (if possible).

6) Decide how significant your results should be. It can be as a percentage when one is greater than the other or as a certain threshold when the value of one option reaches it; that is enough.

7) Make sure you only run one test at a time for any given campaign.

8) Use an A/B testing tool.

9) Test both options at the same time.

10) Give the A/B test enough time to get valuable data.

11) Ask for feedback from real users on why your users behave in specific ways.

12) Focus on your target metric.

The time of general testing can be quite different. Sometimes if there is enough traffic, it can be as little as 24 hours more often. Several days. I am familiar with a case when such research was conducted for several weeks. In my opinion, a typical mistake when defining and preparing a test can be dividing the audience according to specific characteristics, for example, testing one version for the European region and another for Asia, or when users are informed that A/B testing is underway and are asked to view both versions.

A/B testing can be done with mockups in a survey format that is somewhat less effective and is more often used in the early stages of UI design or with the final product, site, or application, creating interactive pages or components for the main and control options. Special applications are integrated into your product to facilitate and automate this process.

Topic 10.6: Usability heuristics

Heuristic evaluation is a process in which experts use rules of thumb to evaluate the usability of user interfaces in independent step-by-step instructions and report problems. Evaluators use established heuristics (e.g., Nielsen-Molich, Norman heuristics) and discover insights that can help design teams improve product usability early in development.

The goals of such testing:

- Identifying problems in the design of a product or service.
- Disclosure of improvement opportunities.
- As well as Studying the behavior and preferences of the target user.

The concept of heuristic analysis is widely used in UX; it is usually one of two options, either using established heuristics or creating your own. The second option allows you to create more flexible and adapted heuristics for a specific product, but it also requires much more time and effort and has a long list of requirements for the experts involved.

How to conduct a heuristic analysis

1) Determine what and how to test. Whether it's the entire product or a single procedure, clearly define the parameters of what to test and the purpose.
2) Define your users and target audience goals, contexts, etc. User personas can help evaluators see things from the users' point of view.
3) Select 3-5 experts, ensuring they have experience and relevant industry.

4) Define heuristics (about 5-10) - this will depend on the nature of the system/product/project.

5) Define heuristics (about 5-10) - this will depend on the nature of the system/product/project.

How to choose experts

To begin with, let's define that the activity is built on the method of expert opinion. Therefore the involvement of several experts is desirable and recommended, and the experience of many projects shows that relatively poor results are achieved if you rely on individual evaluators. If necessary, you can conduct this assessment even by yourself or with the involvement of a minimum number of people. The reason for this is a simple fact, better in a simplified form than not at all. But even in this case, it is desirable that different people carried out the analysis and UI design.

When determining the role of experts, note that they have the following:

- Understand the principles and theory of heuristic analysis.
- Have in-depth knowledge of the domain (topics and specifics of the product).
- Be able to communicate with each other to agree on a list of heuristics.
- Understand the principles of usability and the guidelines of the product platform.

Regarding the number of experts, there is a certain unevenness. Some believe that 2-3 is absolutely enough, considering the total cost of the activity and the fact that it is proportional to the number of involved experts. But some talk about the numbers 5-10. Research by NNGroup shows that when involving up to 5 experts, the area of problem coverage usually does not exceed 75%. Following a normal distribution, at the value of 10 experts, it reaches about

90%. After that, the movement slows down, so when even more experts are involved, the cost still increases proportionally, but the benefits and quality do not change significantly. That is, the optimal value is about 5-7 experts, which is a balance of price and effectiveness.

Nielsen Norman's heuristics

1. Visibility of the system status.

The system should always inform users of what is happening with appropriate feedback within a reasonable time. In other words, we have to play a two-sided game, and all actions must be confirmed by detailed feedback from the system.

2. Match between the system and the real world.

The system should speak the user's language with words, phrases, and concepts familiar to the user, not system-oriented terms. Follow real-world traditions to display information naturally and logically, keeping users' habits, behavior, and mental models in mind.

3. User control and freedom.

Users often choose system functions by mistake and need a marked "emergency exit" to exit an unwanted state without going through an advanced dialog or path. A simple example is a Back button, which allows us to return to the previous menu or undo a specific action during the first 30 seconds if performed accidentally.

4. Consistency and standards.

Users should not wonder if different words, situations, or actions mean the same thing. Follow platform conventions.

5. Error prevention.

A careful design that prevents the problem from occurring is even better than good error messages. Either eliminate error-prone conditions or validate them and allow users to confirm before they take action. It is essential to use it before when the change may be significant or important, and at the same time, quite accidentally made by the user.

6. Recognition rather than recall.

Minimize user memory by making objects, actions, and options visible. The user does not need to remember information from one part of the dialogue to another. Instructions for using the system should be visible or easily accessible when needed. A simple example is captions under the icons in the menu of a mobile application, even if these icons are pretty unambiguous, or hints on complex pages so that the user has fewer questions.

7. Flexibility and efficiency of use.

Accelerators - not visible to the novice user - can often speed up the experience of a power user so that the system can serve both novice and power users. Allow users to adapt frequent actions, depending on the product and type; this can be various kinds of customization for regular users or simplified onboarding for newcomers according to their individual needs, increasing the efficiency and performance of the product through optimization and many others.

8. Aesthetic and minimalist design.

Dialogues should not contain information that is irrelevant or rarely needed. Each additional unit of information in the dialogue competes with the corresponding information units and reduces their relative visibility. This principle can be applied to many areas of the design. To the UI, given the direct style of minimalism and aesthetic presentation, to the content taking into account its weight, and to the UX, given the interaction and complexity of interactions with users.

9. Help users recognize, diagnose, and recover from errors.

Error messages should be expressed in plain language (no codes), accurately identify the problem, and constructively suggest a solution. Each of you can remember a case of using a site or an application when everything suddenly froze or a white screen appeared. It was an error, but you were unaware of how to deal with it.

10. Help and documentation.

Although it is better if the system can be used without documentation, help, and instructions may need to be provided. Any such information should be easy to find and oriented to the user's task.

Module 11: Handout

Topic 11.1: Feasibility

Design thinking methodology uses Desirability, Viability, and Feasibility to test ideas, concepts, and hypotheses to determine whether you have a unique value proposition (called a unique selling point) and are worth pursuing. Not checking these three positions increases risk, cost, and the likelihood of failure. You could say that Desirability, Viability, and Feasibility are risk analysis methodologies for ideas – a set of tools to find the best place for innovation.

Desirability determines: if your product idea has no market value and people don't want or need it, it won't sell. Let's say you can make excellent pitchers, but because they disintegrate when exposed to water or sunlight (that's how bad pitchers are), your users should only keep them in boxes, away from light or water. This means that the typical use of a pitcher for this product will not be relevant, and most likely, the product's desirability will be minimal.

Viability: if your product makes business sense. Even if you have the most desirable product in the world, it is not a good business model if it is too expensive or unprofitable. In the same example with jugs, imagine that you have figured out how to protect them from light and water, but now their cost has increased 500 times, but the probability that they will crack due to water or sunlight is piling up. This is an example of poor viability because the business will not be able to make money selling such expensive jugs.

Feasibility: if your current resources determine whether you can develop a product in the near future. And designers must consider how the product will affect the business.

A feasibility study assesses the practicality of a proposed plan or project. It analyzes project viability to determine whether a project or portfolio is likely to succeed.

For a designer, one of the main criteria in making a final decision regarding an idea or concept is technical feasibility in terms of the technical ability of the team to implement this or that decision. Such an assessment may include the following criteria:

- Complexity.
- Availability of the necessary resources (frameworks, libraries, etc.).
- Availability of required team members (with required level and stack).
- The duration of the task.
- Development complexity (access to necessary elements, systems, etc.).
- Complexity is a relative value defined as a complex factor and not on a particular scale.

Why is it important to remember this?

When creating a product concept or prototype, testing it with users, and validating it with stakeholders, a UX specialist must understand the "reality" of this idea. Although a UX specialist will not directly engage in the development, it is essential to know whether the concepts created can be implemented and understand their relative value. Quite often, there are cases when the designer creates a layout or prototype and approves it with the customer, and then finds out that the team will not be able to reproduce exactly that look or behavior. Then there are conflicts and changes; sometimes, the customer may like a particular decision so much that he does not want to agree to anything else, so our task as designers is to communicate the decision and do it on time.

Sometimes we need to prioritize what we want and can do and compare it with what we need. For example:

Feature A - This can increase site traffic by 10%, but it will take two weeks to implement in development.

Feature B - can improve conversion by 1%, and it takes two days to develop.

Feature C - Can improve conversion by 3% and requires one week of research and one week of development.

Considering Impact and Effort, we can prioritize which features we will introduce. However, avoiding the "idea trap" when the customer approves the concept is impossible. However, as mentioned earlier, we do it not by ourselves, not from the side of the user and business, and we also consider technical features and capabilities.

So how to communicate the technical feasibility and design of the solution

1) Having ideas, concepts, or basic prototypes (even before approval with the customer), you need to schedule a Feasibility Sync.

2) After inviting the production team, conduct a preliminary analysis that involves getting feedback on the new concept from relevant stakeholders.

3) Analyze and question the data obtained in the early stages of the research to ensure that it is reliable.

4) Make an initial "go" or "no go" decision to move forward with the plan, i.e., whether we can make it happen later.

Make feasibility Sync Up regular meetings. They can be planned at the end of each sprint, reviewing what is just being prepared for grooming. Or in a freer format, but with the involvement of technical specialists in the discussion, even before this task is approved by the customer or stakeholders.

Topic 11.2: Buy-in process

The concept of Buy-in is the process of approving and "accepting" the design concept or a specific part of the work. For stakeholders to "support" the project, these people need to be involved in the decision-making process.

Buy-in is more than just a "like" for your design. This requires a fundamental understanding of the project's goals and the metrics that will determine success, as well as agreement on the implementation or execution of any solution created.

Stakeholder buy-in increases the success rate of your project! When your internal stakeholders are involved, the project's complexity becomes better. And in general, the entire project management process is much smoother and often more collaborative.

Whether you are a project team leader, a designer, or a consultant, you will inevitably interact with stakeholders and need to provide them with information that will help the team move forward as planned.

Buy-in or approval can be determined at the levels of internal stakeholders or considered more globally with external ones. In any organization, there are two types of stakeholders.

Internal stakeholders are those people who work directly in the business, including owners, managers, employees, and board members or trustees. Internal stakeholders tend to generate ideas for the business and are more likely to support them almost immediately because they understand the decisions' impact on the business's bottom line.

External stakeholders are outside the business but interact with it in a certain way. These include customers, community members, and suppliers who provide goods or services to the business. For example, depending on the type of project, these may be consultants or engineers who are not directly related to the project but may be involved in the initial setup of the infrastructure or environment. The classification of internal and external stakeholders is quite simple but somewhat conditional; if a person or a group of people is not directly involved in creating a product, or is not part of a team, most likely these are external stakeholders, or they are not at all.

First, you must prepare artifacts, mockups, prototypes, research results, testing, and other results, presenting which you can better explain a particular decision and motivation.

Next, you need to plan a meeting; sometimes, it's pretty simple: choose a time on the calendar for a particular day, and send an invitation. Sometimes it is necessary to involve external and internal stakeholders, schedule a meeting several weeks in advance, agree, etc. It all depends on the standards of the company or on your project.

Then - we conduct a presentation with an explanation of the concept, advocacy of the solution, and other elements to present the idea. Leave plenty of time for discussion and questions from stakeholders. Next, they can vote, accept/reject/send the concept for revision. Sometimes the weight of the voice of one stakeholder can be higher than the sum of others.

But as a result, we will either transfer the approved concept to development, refine it, or even change it significantly. Sometimes there may be several such sessions. Depending on the complexity of the process and the number of stages or levels of approval, the entire process can take from one hour, i.e., the duration of one meeting, to several sprints, i.e., two weeks or more. It mainly depends on the process and the complexity of the functionality because if we are talking about approving a new placement of a button or a specific component on the screen, it will most likely be simple and fast, but if it concerns complex flows, changes and approvals can take quite a long time.

Topic 11.3: Presentation

Sooner or later (preferably early and regularly), every mockup, prototype, or in general, the design of the solution needs to be presented to the team and the client. The main tasks are:

- Communication of decisions.
- Presentation of concepts.
- Discussion and identification of areas for improvement.
- Approval.

The first common mistake is expecting your decision to be accepted and approved the first time. It does happen, but if you're planning to do it, you're putting yourself under high stress. And in fact, as mentioned before, although we try to minimize mistakes, it is not a bad thing, so you need to be ready for criticism or changes. All proposals are rarely accepted the first time because the initial mock-ups or concepts are usually raw and must go through several validation stages.

Principles of good design presentation

1) "Beautiful does not mean useful. Show the statistics." Often it is not enough for the client to see an exciting or aesthetic picture, even if it meets all the requirements. Be prepared to communicate the decision in numbers: conversion rate, metrics, number of positive reviews, test results, etc.

2) Every design should have a measurable goal. Show that you can (could) achieve yours. This abstract goal can be tied to company goals, product goals, or your team's milestones. Show that you have reached the goal that was set for this task.

3) Show the process. You don't need to describe in detail every activity that you did. Still, you must show the customer that the idea, concept, or in general, "solution" you present did not arise by chance and that it is the result of work, research, and other activities that help you justify this decision.

Also, while working on the presentation, pay attention to its requirements, whether an informal meeting or a rather bureaucratic procedure. Think about whom you are creating it for.

At the beginning of each presentation - prepare the audience. Often, your listeners may not fully understand the essence of the meeting and why they were invited. When planning a presentation, briefly describe in the invitation letter precisely what will be discussed at the meeting, why, and your goals.

At the beginning of the meeting, briefly state the plan, and describe the problem you were solving or the tasks you faced. Start with the results, and then move on to the details of your processes or activities.

Prepare a basis for discussion, if provided. Build your story in a way that will keep everyone interested. The ability to make successful presentations comes with experience; some people feel as comfortable as possible communicating with others and "holding a punch," while others can be nervous. It is essential to practice presenting unsuccessful ideas or work because it happens often, but it is not the end of the world.

We are not talking about lousy performance but actually about a negative result. For example, you conducted a study and found that one of your main hypotheses is wrong.

How to present an unsuccessful result

1) First, justify the task you performed, what the motivation was, and the expected result.

2) Tell the team what result you got (what went wrong or why you consider it harmful).

3) Use the negative outcome factors to articulate what you learned in this exercise. Explain why even a negative result can bring you success (in the example with a hypothesis, this means that you disproved it early enough when you did not spend many resources on product development).

4) Outline the next steps you will take to apply these results and make your product better. You can use them in your work or write a whole action plan for the team.

Another critical skill is coping with an adverse reaction or confrontation. This is especially necessary for beginners who have not yet learned to abstract from their work and fall in love with intermediate results.

Imagine the situation: you have created mockups or even a full prototype for a very cool project, elaborate, detailed, and aesthetic; you have been working on it for the last month or two, confidently formed all the materials and artifacts into a presentation, and conducted it for stakeholders. But, after the presentation, you receive negativity, criticism, and dissatisfaction instead of enthusiastic applause for your skill or just pleasant comments on the work that took a lot of time and effort. How will you behave in this situation?

In many cases, one or more stakeholders may be dissatisfied with the outcome or believe that the task was not completed correctly or as planned. This is not normal, but very typical. In such a situation, you can't just accept criticism. It is necessary to discuss it and, using methods of analysis, to communicate possible solutions.

Ask the stakeholder to:

- Explain what exactly he considers unsuccessful.
- Give an example or explain your vision of how these activities could be successful.
- Communicate with them, and don't take criticism as a given.

Stakeholders are also living people; unfortunately, our personal problems, character, or, let's be honest, not very developed soft skills can affect how we express our dissatisfaction. However, any such situation can be resolved through proper response and communication. Just as in the UX process, we do not grab the first thought or idea that comes to our mind to solve a problem, so in communication with customers and working with criticism or dissatisfaction, we need to find the truth and the root cause and ways to improve the situation.

Topic 11.4: Design Pitch

A pitch is a great way to communicate your idea, how it works, why it matters, and whom it benefits. And in the process of creating it, you'll refine the critical elements of your idea and the way you talk about them. A presentation is a primary way you'll present your idea and use it to convince different types of people - from customers to prospects - to support your idea.

When creating a pitch, use the principle of three circles, starting from the cause to the result:

- Why? - The reason. What is the reason? Why did you do that? What goals did you pursue? It is best to address business goals or talk about well-known tasks without going into design jargon.
- How? - Process. In what way? How did you decide that? What processes or activities did you follow? You do not need to describe the entire process, let

alone explain the specifics of the activities, but it is important to focus on the details that most influenced the proposed concept, such as research or how exactly you validated the assumptions.

- What? - Result. What did you achieve? How does this solve the original problem?

- Sometimes you can add the 4th factor, "And?" or "Next," where you can describe your next steps or explain what you learned.

Topic 11.5: Preparation design for a handout

When submitting designs for development, we have to prepare them and "clean" them from the garbage typically formed in the design process. Since developers have access to design files filled with dozens of unfinished frames, iterations, components, etc., it makes sense to communicate which parts of the files are ready for implementation and which are still being worked on. It is necessary to prepare and transfer components (images, icons, etc.) that developers may not be able to download independently.

For designers, this process is essential, although typically, many forget or ignore it, relegating it to the background. But:

- This mechanism of transfer of ready-made layouts simplifies the task of developers.

- Minimizes rework and errors.

- Helps to improve communication between designers and developers.

- Improves file navigation.

Preparing artifacts for a handout

1) Cleaning is based on cleaning or organizing your files before giving them to developers. It is not an exception when many concepts are intermediate or incomplete in the design process, but they can be helpful, so we do not delete them. The 2nd stage - Navigation - is based on the possibility or impossibility of finding specific information, layouts, or building logical connections in the materials you transfer. This leads to the first tip:

Use predefined naming and semantics when naming pages and components. Add tags, emojis, and page titles to indicate what is ready for implementation. This does not mean that you should delete all previous iterations. However, try to organize your space so that developers don't have to wonder which version is final.

2) Give styles appropriate and descriptive names. Add component documentation to your design system. Contributors can use the Go to Main Component feature to learn more about its usage, but developers cannot:

- Name layers and components based on their IDs.
- Add meaningful descriptions to components.
- Know when and how can contributors use any options or states; accessibility and contrast guidelines.

If you don't have enough time for a full-fledged UI kit, or even more so a system design, try to at least build essential documentation for the most specific or customized components to avoid questions or guesswork in the development team.

3) If you use a lot of icons, images, or other graphic materials, export them and form them into one folder or archive. This will make it easier for developers to extract these materials. Use the same semantics when naming them. Example: *icon/solid/star/24,*

so that anyone who uses it immediately understands that this component is 1) an icon, 2) solid - it is filled, 3) a star is an asterisk, 4) and the size is 24px.

This kind of semantics is not mandatory; you can adapt it to your needs or complexity because, for example, there is a concept of the style of the solid icon, i.e., filled; this is relevant for projects that have two or more styles, say filled, linear and colored icons. If you do not have one, it is unnecessary to use it. Choose for yourself; the main thing is that it is:

- Understandable.

- Consistently.

- The whole team supported this format.

- Logically, you are not faced with making super long titles, but you need to make them understandable.

4) For components, don't forget to add states. This may not be necessary at the prototyping stage, but it will be essential for developers. After all, most components have more than one default state.

Typically, three states can be considered:

Default - standard

Hover - pointing the mouse

Disabled - unavailable

Depending on which components you work with, you will need to consider different states; sometimes, there may be only two default and disabled ones. You also need to create separate or adapt components for mobile.

5) Add notes and explanations to avoid mistakes. If some specific interactions or components behave atypically, add notes to minimize misunderstandings and rework.

6) Check contrast and other accessibility details before you submit mockups. Sometimes, additional checks are necessary, even if you have planned color combinations at the beginning.

7) Optimize images and icons. It is often possible to buy or download huge images. This is great for quality but bad for system performance (i.e., context deployment time, downloads, traffic, etc.).

Topic 11.6: Design Documentation

Design documentation is a collection of documents and resources covering all product development aspects. Documentation should include information about users, product features, project implementation timelines; all important implementation details; and design solutions your team and stakeholders agreed upon.

Documentation can be created at different stages of the project. Sometimes, teams choose to delay and write documentation at the end of the project. This can be a dangerous approach. The lack of complete documentation confuses the stage of project implementation. It is best to divide the documentation into stages according to the design process and record the work with the documentation as an essential activity of each sprint. This will give all team members a better understanding of every decision and every step.

Different projects may have different views on documentation; some require full detail, others only superficial. However, it is essential because:

1. The documentation serves to clarify the requirements.

We create it not only for actual documentation but also for approval. Getting stakeholder approval to start a project is one of the most critical steps in the design process, and it's much easier and better to do it in documents rather than letters or verbally. Documentation helps you to organize and communicate your thinking to your stakeholders, which in turn helps them to understand how your design solutions will meet the needs of your users and their own business goals.

2. Documentation will allow you to see fine points in the process and optimize them.

By documenting the project, you also help in its implementation. Product design is a collaborative process, and in many cases, multiple people work on a project. It's not always possible to share implementation details verbally (for example, when working with remote teams). In this way, project documents are a single source of truth for everyone involved in product development and rally your team around a specific goal.

3. Although documentation is sometimes routine, accuracy and clarity are motivating.

Good documentation communicates the product at a high level and gets team members excited about the vision. It answers the question, "How do we want to build it?" and, importantly, "Why do we want to build it?".

Documentation helps establish a shared vision and minimizes individual interpretation.

I divide all documentation into three types. This is my classification, so it may differ slightly from the information presented by other authors and designers. Still, it seems to me to be intuitive and easy to remember, so I am sharing it with you.

1) Product-related documentation. It describes goals, objectives, vision, potential users, competitors, etc.

2) Project documentation. It explains the design processes, describes the composition of the team and features and areas of responsibility, determines how this or that task should be done, and the results are presented.

3) Documentation related to the design of solutions. It may include a design system, style guide, explanation of patterns, rules for using components, description of design activities, and their results.

Classification of documentation does not have a direct correlation to how often and on which projects it is used, but from my practice, documentation related to the design of solutions is still the most popular, and you can find the most materials and resources about it on the Internet.

What if there is no documentation on a project?

The answer might not impress you, but - to create. Unfortunately, there is no universal set of templates and templates that you can apply because, in many cases, what others use may not suit you. In the case of creating documentation, you need to remember that it is an iterative and cyclical process, few documents are created permanently, and most of them you will have to update and maintain for quite some time. If you don't have anything at all, start by defining the space where you will store information, it can be something more primitive like Notion or more profile products like Confluence.

Start with Process Mapping.

It is essential to study the current process and document it to change or improve it.

The second step is standardization - Templates, rules - describe them. Work-related and product-related (such as patterns).

Then the third step is the Documentation of the research and results. You can create a single template that can be reused for different artifacts.

Between the absence and availability of even essential documentation, I choose documentation. Still, I would choose less between creating many files and documents because it is necessary and 1-2 documents related to the process or design of artifacts because each created document requires support and, therefore, an investment of time.

Module 12: Portfolio

Topic 12.1: UX portfolio

Let's start with the difference between UI and UX portfolios, as it is pretty significant:

UI	UX
Focuses on visual design	Focuses on processes
Shows images of screens or layout states may include animations and other types of interaction, and visualizations.	Shows images of screens only in the format of visual content, and mostly focuses on artifacts related to the project, for example, the process you followed, the research you conducted, you can present maps, reports, activity plans.
Activities related to the development of visual style, branding, work with style guides, or UI components.	Activities involve research, analysis, idea generation, prototyping, testing, and more.

When you plan the portfolio's structure or its content, pay attention to specialization because many examples of portfolios on the Internet are presented precisely as UI portfolios. They have little information, processes and activities are not described, and there are no logically described cases.

A few principles of a good UX portfolio:

- Stick to the point. Use strong copywriting to showcase your talent and put essential messages first clearly.
- Prove your worth and qualifications - show where and when you qualified, including results. Likewise, demonstrate good UX practices: everything you include should support your expertise.
- Balance your tone. Describe what fits well with the work culture you prefer, highlighting your passion in the context of Teamwork Skills.

When presenting the project in the portfolio, including

- Its name
- Description of the client
- Tasks or challenges
- Description of the process
- Achievement
- Artifacts and visual solutions
- Sometimes you can also mention what you learned

How to create a cool portfolio

1) Start with a little intro. Briefly describe yourself, your experience, and your specialty, and leave your contacts.
2) Select the 3-4 best, most relevant examples for your desired role. (If the projects are too small, you can take 5-6, but keep in mind that the total number should not be too voluminous). When choosing projects, select those that best characterize you as a professional, have different stages of the design process, and are about which you can tell the details.

3) Describe each project in terms of the processes and activities that YOU did. There is no need to talk about what the team did, do not focus on the stages of development; it should be the design of the portfolio itself.

4) Choose a structure or collect template pages that you can use for each project.

5) Focus on project challenges or achievements. For example, I often describe the state of the project or product when I started and finished working with it or the specifics of the work.

Make sure that your portfolio meets the requirements and needs of the job. For example, if it's a general position, include web, mobile, and examples of different platforms and domains. If the position is in the banking sector, and you have a fintech product - put it first in the portfolio.

Pay attention to

- **Visual design.** Even when you are a UX designer, the visual design of the entire portfolio should be up to par. Remember grids, consistency, color combinations, and composition.

- **Accessibility.** If accessibility is in the requirements of your job or in the list of skills, but your portfolio does not correspond to it, poor contrasts, low-quality images, and small fonts are evil. Attention will be drawn to it, and there will be questions, or the impression will be spoiled.

- **Processes.** A UX designer needs to describe processes and understand them correctly. Please note exactly what was done, why, and how the results were applied.

- **The overall quality of the content.** Images should not be pixelated and text with errors. You should also not leave the text with placeholders like lorem ipsum; it is better to come up with your own copy or at least beat the content so that the text fish does not catch the eye. As for mistakes in the text, this is a separate topic that can be talked about a lot, but the easiest way is to present your portfolio to friends and colleagues or read the portfolio yourself several times: when you create it, a few days after and a week later. Initially, you will not see many mistakes because you are not reading but scanning the text, but other people who do not know what you wrote about, or even you, but after a specific time, will be able to look at it from a different angle and make the necessary changes.

The portfolio is another one of the products you are developing - it should be top-notch!

What not to add to your portfolio

1) Projects with which your negativity is connected.

"Yes, it's terrible, I didn't want to do it, but the customer said so."

Don't blame the client, the team, the budget, or anyone else if you're not proud of the project - don't add it to the portfolio.

2) Projects you don't want to repeat.

"- You have impressive logos. Our company needs a logo.

- I don't make logos anymore."

A portfolio is a menu, and everything you present is available.

3) Projects that were copied (even for educational purposes). The design world is pretty small, and there is quite a high chance that somebody may know the owner or recognize the work from Dribbble or Behance, which might kill all your chances of obtaining the job.

4) Old simple projects that don't reflect the expertise and can worsen the impression.

Even before the meeting with the candidate, the team or the interviewer who will conduct the technical interview gets acquainted with the portfolio. Based on it, a particular impression is formed about you as a specialist, techniques, skills, and accuracy in work. Often what you add will depend on the questions you may get. Usually, interviewers form a list of questions based on a portfolio. Therefore, it is helpful to carry out the following exercise: when you create a portfolio, wait a few days, open it, and try to write 20 questions that the interviewers could ask you based on it. After a day or two, do it again and again. Your goal is to get 60 questions, or as many as possible before you run out of ideas. Next, think about whether you can answer them; if not - prepare or remove this information from the portfolio altogether.

How to make your portfolio stand out

To stand out among other candidates, you can expand your portfolio with additional information by including:

Certifications. If you have been trained and have specialized certifications. You can also use certifications in related specialties (for example, in FE, business analysis, branding, or graphic design).

Non-project activities. Because often, in addition to commercial projects, many designers participate in additional activities. Talk about them (for example, hackathons, charity projects, educational projects, mentoring, coaching, and others). Projects related to design will also look fantastic; for example, if you have your product or if you have participated in the creation of another physical or digital product as a manager, this is interesting because it shows your skills in planning, communication, and management, which can also be helpful.

Topic 12.2: Why some portfolios don't work

Mistake 1. Some portfolios don't work because they don't have a specific goal

Your portfolio should have a purpose. This will guide your decisions, from what to include in your portfolio to the text you'll include, your choice of platform, and more. So when you're creating a portfolio, ask yourself: What do I want users to do when they receive it? Do I want them to contact me about work? Do I want them to subscribe to my newsletter? Do I want to connect with them on Behance or Dribbble?

When you have a specific goal in mind, you can identify the steps you need to take with your portfolio to help you achieve it. The goal can be different, for example, to get a job for a specific vacancy, and I say "specific", because a universal portfolio is a rarity. Or you want to highlight your expertise and teach works; this is another, more social option.

Mistake 2. The portfolio does not work because you turned it into a collection of works

Don't showcase absolutely everything you've done. Think of your portfolio as your resume. You want to tell the story of your career by showcasing only the best you have to offer. This means including the things you're proud of and leaving the rest behind the scenes. For example, that webpage you created for a class project in college might have been pretty cool at the time - but is it something you want to show off now in your career? On the other hand, if you've just developed a design that impressed your employers and helped your users, then that's something you should include!

Mistake 3. Bad portfolios can be that way because of the loss of relevance; they are not updated. Created once and for all

To give potential clients and users a better idea of who you are and what kind of work you do, your portfolio should always include recent work. This means that you include recent projects that you are proud of and ones relevant to the types of clients you want to attract. After all, you want a portfolio reflecting your current talent and skill level, not years ago. Remember my dream job story; portfolio relevance is always important.

Mistake 4. The portfolio does not show YOU. Your style, your skills

It's important to stay professional when creating your portfolio, but you shouldn't be afraid to add a bit of your personality. This can take many forms, including how you write, design your website, and even the projects you choose to feature. Sometimes these are minor details, footnotes, interesting facts about you and your work process, or other information that will help you stand out from the competition. Templates and very templated portfolios from the Internet work the worst in this regard. After all, many people want to see YOU as a specialist, not whether you know how to use Google search well.

Individuality helps to remind potential clients that you are also a person - and maybe someone is quite fun and unconventional, someone, on the contrary, is very serious, but you, like many other professionals, have your own vision and style, which is quite essential. Make the portfolio yours, consistent, concrete, not just a collection of trends and pictures, detailed, exciting, and showing your skill.

Other portfolio mistakes are usually less significant but are still noticed by many:

- Grammatical errors.
- Using informal vocabulary or language.
- Too many graphics and elements.
- Too minimalist presentation of information, do not confuse it with minimalism in general; here, we are talking about short titles, images without context, etc.
- Quite painful for interviewers is the option when the portfolio is only a link to Figma that is not structured as a portfolio; that is, it is just a set of artboards with some designs or on GoogleDisk from which interviewers need to download something.
- Also, check if there are any broken links in the portfolio; when you can't go to the page, there is nothing, or the contact is protected.
- A typical mistake to avoid is using overly primitive templates.
- And the most critical thing, for many, especially for me, is when I look at someone's portfolio, which includes copied projects or works. And we are not talking about modifications when you offer an alternative version of the design for a particular product, namely, when you reproduce someone's style or someone's design solution, make small changes and consider it now your project.

Topic 12.3: How to prepare for a UX interview

A technical interview is for any position related to the technology industry, such as information technology. Technical interviews can be held over the phone, online, or in person, and can last anywhere from one hour to a full day. Interview questions include traditional questions, puzzles, technical training tests, and problem-solving questions. There is no single format or standard for an interview in the IT industry, specifically in UX design. There are details you can find in almost all companies, but there are also things that each can do differently.

Technical interviews are divided into several stages, for example:

- General
- Group
- Interviews with the project representative

Before the interview, when you have just sent your CV and portfolio to the vacancy, there is a screening and reviewing of the portfolio and CV, which determines whether you are an excellent candidate to participate in the interview.

During the interview: everything starts with an intro, where the interviewer will talk about the process, and you can introduce yourself, followed by technical questions about the design process, activities, your experience, etc. There may be a discussion of projects from the portfolio, specific technical tasks, or situations you will be asked to solve. Also, in almost 100% of interviews, there will be a specific language test, usually English, but it depends on the language of the project you are applying for. In the end, there will usually be a Q&A part where you will be invited to ask your questions.

After the interview: You will receive feedback (written or verbal), and sometimes you will be offered an additional test task; if the interviewer has doubts or wants to see how you cope with a real problem, if all stages are successfully completed, you will be invited on Offer-talk, where they will discuss the conditions that can be offered to you in the event of employment.

Four types of interviews

1) Behavioral questions.

Technical interviews usually start like any other: with a series of general and behavioral questions designed to learn more about the candidate and how he or she will fit into the company's culture.

2) Situational questions.

After asking a few behavioral and skill questions, the interviewer can move on to a few situational interview questions in which they present you with a hypothetical situation and ask how you would solve the problem or react to it. With these questions, the interviewer wants to know if you have anticipated specific workplace problems that may arise and how you would have responded to them. For example, you may be offered a problem and asked how you will deal with it, say if you have a conflict with a customer or manager or do not know how to do a specific task.

3) Experience and trainings.

When an interviewer asks about your education, they want to know about your specific technical training and education and how it has prepared you for the position you are applying for. When answering these questions, mention any special certifications, coursework, and training you've received, as well as any academic achievements related to the position you're applying for.

4) The questions are related to the skills and knowledge required to perform the job.

Usually, these are technical, theoretical, or descriptive questions directly related to the tasks that will need to be performed in this role.

How to prepare for an interview

1. Get your portfolio in order.

If you haven't already, ensure your portfolio is in top shape. How is it put in order? First of all, it is ready for presentation, you have added new and removed irrelevant projects in it, and it also fits the employer's needs (if an interview for a project with Mobile, the portfolio must contain projects with Mobile). In general, it is relevant; that is, all projects are relatively recent.

Advice:

Sort the projects in your portfolio in order of importance, or in the order in which you would like to see them. There are times when older works are not reviewed, so prioritize. You can also use the wow factor and not so wow factor. If you have a super cool project that you're proud of, you can put it first, even if it's not the newest.

---

2. Think and, if necessary, practice the story about yourself.

Even though the question "Tell me about yourself" is very simple, it usually causes the most stress. The story about yourself should not exceed 3-5 minutes. You should not start too globally; the interviewer is interested in relevant work experience, not what year you graduated from school.

Advice:

Correctly building a self-presentation, you will be able to manage the interview in a certain way, and set the tone for it. By mentioning certain domains with which you worked, or special activities, you will make the interviewer want to ask you about them in more detail. But please do not use this advice too much.

---

3. Review the theory and fundamental concepts.

Often, it is the basic concepts that are problematic. So, when working with them, we focus more on the practical than the theoretical component.

Check out the theory for:

- Processes
- Activities
- Basic principles of UX
- Guidelines for the design of different platforms

and other. Pay attention to those mentioned in the job description.

4. Do a little research on the company you are interviewing for.

Check out her website, projects, and information on the Internet. Learn basic information about the activity. Prepare a few questions you would be interested in receiving from a company representative.

Advice:

Formulate a "motivation" for why you want to join the company. This is another question that quite often puts us in a dead end. It should be something real, not abstract. Think about what you need, what you would like to have in an ideal office or job, what team you would like, how to develop, etc. Next, try to map, that is, to combine your expectations with what the company has, in a certain way this will be your motivation. Sometimes they answer this question too directly and say that they are interested in a high salary. I am somewhat skeptical about this, although I have colleagues who, on the contrary, positively perceive it as honesty.

Most technical interviews are relatively straightforward, you just need to understand the mechanics of it, and prepare for the specific arrangements, based on the position description, your experience level, and screening questions that you might have been asked before the actual interview..

Make sure you familiarize yourself with the job and review the relevant theory if necessary. Don't worry; this is just a conversation with a fellow UXer.

- Be ready to turn on the camera when you come to the interview and present your portfolio.
- Don't be late. Many companies have a rule of 10-15 minutes, after which the interview is canceled or postponed.

STAR method

The STAR method is an interviewing technique that gives you a simple format to tell a story by setting out the situation, the task, the action, and the outcome.

S - Situation: Set the scene and provide the necessary details of your example.

T - Task: Describe what your responsibility was in this situation.

A - Action: Explain the steps you took to resolve the problem.

R - Result: Share the results your actions have achieved.

Using these four components to shape your answer makes it much easier to give the interviewer an "accessible but compelling narrative."

Question markers in which it is appropriate to use STAR:

- Tell me about a time when…
- What do you do when…
- Have you ever…
- Give me an example…
- Describe the situation…

Using this method is also beneficial for the portfolio itself.

Topic 12.4: Tricky questions on a UX interview

"Tell us how you develop as a designer."

When asking this question, the interviewer wants to hear that you are developing and not just stopping at this point. Development is not always directly related to books, so you can talk about your training programs, projects, podcasts you listen to, or other activities that help us to become better designers. Often this question puts many in shock because all the names and authors of books fly out of their heads, and various articles, podcasts, or YouTube channels are not always suitable for the answer. Therefore, before the interview, think so that you can answer. I always have 2-3 books of different levels prepared (one on UI, one on product strategy, and my favorite design author) that I remember well in case of something I can quickly name. Also, for some interviewers, reading books is directly related to the level because beginners most often read articles or listen to podcasts to get the gist, and more advanced and experienced ones read books and form their own gist, notes, and insights.

"Tell me about a case when everything did not go as planned," or "Tell me about the case when your decision was wrong."

Such questions are asked to understand how you cope with problems or unexpected situations. They are also often stressful because when time is limited, it is difficult to think of an accurate answer or choose an appropriate situation in the interview environment. In your answer, describe the situation, what exactly went wrong, how you reacted to it, and how it ended. I disagree with the advice of some specialists that it is necessary to take some straightforward situations that end with a happy ending. I once did so, but at this stage of my career, I understand that it looks untrue. Even if the situation ended badly, it is not critical, and you can talk about it because the purpose of the task is to understand how you reacted and how exactly you could fix it. If you didn't do it at the time, describe how you would hypothetically do it and what you learned. Three situations that I do not recommend talking about: those that are related to legal grounds, for example, the company was fined by the court for your mistake; and those that are not explicitly related to you, for example, on our project the developers did such and such; and those that do not have a logical conclusion or continue now or are related to your job change, for example, and here, just last week, we did such and such, and now I am forced to look for a new job.

"What made you start working in UX design."

There is also no correct answer to this question; for the interviewer, it is not so important to know whom you worked for before design, why you decided to change your profession, etc., as it is to understand your general motivation. Therefore, I do not recommend spending 10 minutes telling how, for example, you went to art school or drew well, but you need to outline why you chose to design and UX in particular. As a follow-up to this, there may often be questions about the processes or activities, or stages of the design process that you like the most. And again, it's not the answer that matters; it's the context and your train of thought. Including information relevant to design or enriching your expertise with skills that can be applied in design is essential. For example, if you have a technical background or experience in project management, have worked in graphic design and are proficient with tools and graphic editors, or have skills in IT areas such as business analysis, testing, or development.

"What is your greatest weakness."

This is the most difficult of the issues that we are currently considering. Some recommend naming things that are not directly related to your work. Some say it is necessary to talk about features, the negative of which you can cover with positive. There is no definite solution here, but it is something that you need to think about in advance so that you don't talk nonsense later because part of your job is perseverance and attention to detail. You say you are as active as possible and ignore the details - that's bad. On the other hand, if you explain that you are active, that is why it is a little difficult for you to sit still. Still, it is easy to communicate with people; it is a little better because, in the work of a UX designer, you will often communicate.

"What excites you most about this position."

The company representative wants to understand your motivation and interest in a specific position here. Often, people are actively looking for a job, submit dozens of resumes, and attend many interviews; the driver of this is the need for employment. However, some employers want to see you motivated to work for them and understand that they are not just another company on your interview list. For this, you need to understand where and for which project you are going. What exactly is excellent for you in this company? For example, company one may have an excellent social package, company two - cool foreign projects, company three -a team, and company four - opportunities for continuous learning. For yourself, you choose what is most valuable to you, but it is also essential to talk about it to employers. After all, even if you don't know the exact conditions in the company, you need to outline what is necessary for you to work successfully. I don't think the answer "Friends recommended me" is perfect because it is very superficial. Although the company is pleased that it is recommended to others, your motivation is not visible here. Therefore, it is advisable to think about it in advance.

Topic 12.5: Design Critique

A Design Critic or Critical analysis is performed to evaluate the design and provide feedback on whether it meets business goals and user needs. Design critiques encourage team collaboration and create a positive team culture to improve design ideas. Feedback from design critiques helps designers think outside the box, often leading to better, more innovative solutions throughout the design process.

Running a productive design critique session can be challenging. Designers often forget that not everyone understands the intricacies of the design process, the language of design criticism, and its rules. Therefore, sometimes such sessions, without proper preparation, are tough. Your job is to educate the audience, provide constructive criticism, and do it right.

A design critique can be a one-time event when you need feedback from a customer or team or a regular activity. Three roles are distinguished among its participants when it comes to design criticism as an event.

The one who presents. This is the lead designer who created and will present the design work on behalf of the design team. This person is responsible for showing the final stage of the design process and providing all the necessary context and content for the critique. For example, he/she will probably be responsible for conducting research and preparing design decisions made at this stage.

The facilitator will help enforce the rules of the design critique and ensure that all participants follow them. He/she is responsible for keeping the discussion on topic, schedule, and time. The facilitator's job is to remind everyone of the main question to be answered during the critique, and if the conversation begins to stray from the focus of the discussion, to intervene on tangents. Sometimes the facilitator will record notes and, as a result, summarize all theses from the meeting.

Critics. The primary audience for the critique session will be critics. The critical group should include 5-7 other team members (designers, developers, copywriters, product managers, etc.) and relevant business stakeholders. The primary responsibility of the critics is to provide feedback on the design within the rules and to help improve the presented solution. It is essential to understand that critics do not necessarily have to specialize in design or development. Still, they should have enough knowledge and skills to provide a thorough critique and be able to explain it.

How to hold a design critique?

1) Decide what is being presented. What level of quality will be presented? Will it be a desktop or mobile experience? What usage scenarios should be considered? Is there any previous work that should be shared beforehand to provide context?

2) Based on this, we can think about Whom to invite. Who are the most relevant team members and business stakeholders? How many perspectives do you need to include to get a complete design critique?

267

3) And as a result, let's share Who will perform the key roles. Who will be the presenter, facilitator, and note-taker? How will the results of the critique session be captured and shared with the rest of the team after the session?

Make sure the business goals are clear and understandable. What problem is the business trying to solve with these designs? Articulate the client's goal using a statement about the work to be done: "As a type of user, I want to have a specific purpose of having a specific reason." Use job story or user story formats, which we have already learned about earlier.

Rules of design critique

1) First, when presenting a solution or criticism, Be prepared. Don't say, "I'm not sure about this decision." Explain clearly why you think it won't work.

2) It is essential to build logical connections, First problems, then solutions. Take a step back and discuss issues and questions about the current design. Do not accept criticism as a permanent phenomenon, even if it comes from very high-level stakeholders, discuss.

3) Be specific. Organize feedback so that it is as straightforward as possible; explain what works and what doesn't.

4) Be straightforward. Tell us what you think about the design. Being vague or overly sensitive won't help here.

5) Don't criticize the person or the process; criticize the decision. Make suggestions, not demands.

Closing words

Starting a new profession is never easy, whether you're newly graduated or transitioning from another sphere. The key to a successful process is to begin and move gradually, planned. We would all like it to be easy to acquire skills or a profession, take an online course, or watch a couple of lessons and get an incredible job. In general, if you look superficially - we can do so because the course or book can give us basic knowledge or theory, but there is much work, effort, and time behind the scenes. Understanding that effort is required for the result is essential. When we invest a lot of time and effort to master a specific skill or gain experience, we better perceive the result and achievement; we understand that this is our achievement and not an accidental success. And also, we know more clearly when we can get them.

This handbook is intended to provide a steady base for everyone who wants or has started in UX design, but mainly to encourage everyone to move forward. One book, course, or video is never enough; life is constantly learning. Lifelong learning is an indispensable tool for every career and organization. In the IT field, as in many others, your drive and willingness to self-learn are crucial. **Learn, read, practice. Create your own "database" and every day become better than the day before.**

Glossary

■ Activity - any processes involving actions and a final result. Activities are used for: information search, product creation, communication, etc.

■ Analysis - the detailed review and processing of something's information, elements, or structure. It involves processing to obtain additional information or expand existing information.

■ Artifact - something (document, information, prototype, etc.) observed in a study or experiment that is not natural but occurs due to a preparatory or research procedure. In other words, it is the result of work that can be presented or applied.

■ Assumptions - what you assume is true, even without evidence. Assumptions are formed on certain input information but can be considered fact only after verification. Assumptions can also be called hypotheses or suppositions; we expect that any hypothesis should be tested, confirmed, or refuted.

■ Business analyst (BA) - help companies to improve processes, products, services, and software through data analysis.

■ Back-end developer (BE) - creates and maintains mechanisms that process data and perform website actions. Unlike front-end (FE) developers, who control everything you see on a website, BE developers are involved in data storage, security, and other server-side functions that you don't see.

■ A client is a person or company that is a customer of product creation services. Usually, this is a role with great responsibility and opportunities.

■ Content - information content of product pages (text, images, graphics, etc.). Content is usually created by copywriters and provided to the designer. In some cases, UX specialists create content - a separate branch of design - UX Writing.

- Discovery - a stage in the UX-design process characterized by activities aimed at familiarization with the product or its requirements, research, analysis of the existing product, or others.

- Edge case - a problem or situation that occurs only at the highest or lowest end of the range of possible values or in extreme situations. For example: from the given range of 1-100, the user chose 0. Surnames in some countries can consist of 3 or more words.

- Empty state - a concept used in the planning and creating of a product and involves system states in which data cannot be stored. For example, Table not filled, 404: page error, Information not loaded, etc.

- Estimation - the process of estimating the duration or cost of the task.

- Feedback - information about reactions to the product, the person's task performance, etc., is used as a basis for improvement.

- The framework is a solution infrastructure that facilitates the development of complex systems, that is, a specific template or format that helps systematize processes.

- Front-end developer (FE) - architects and develops websites and applications using web technologies.

- Glyph - used in design, architecture, and typography, defines a simple sign, mark, or symbol that has a specific meaning and is used to indicate.

- Grooming or refinement is a Scrum team meeting where tasks for the next sprint or another piece of work are discussed and estimated. Grooming involves keeping information about product tasks and goals up to date, estimating and prioritizing activities, and preparing the team for the next sprints.

■ Guidelines - instructions that guide through a process or task. They give general guidance on completing a task or advice on how to act in a situation. They usually give a good overview of how to proceed when no specific policy or standard exists. It can be used to explain how to perform a specific task, carry out a particular activity, or correctly create prototypes and designs for a particular platform.

■ A mental model explains a person's thinking process about how something works in the real world. This is the perception of the surrounding world, the relationships between its various parts, and a person's intuitive perception of his own actions and their consequences.

■ A milestone is a specific point in the project's life cycle or the product as a whole, which is used to measure progress toward the final goal.

■ MVP - Minimum Viable Product is a version of the product with enough features to be used by early customers who can then provide feedback for future improvements.

■ Placeholder - a name or text fragment added to the input field to tell users exactly what content or type of text they need to enter.

■ Prejudice is a bias in favor of or against one person or group, especially in a way that is considered unfair. In design, it is a judgment of the success or failure of a product or a specific solution based on one's own vision, not on the business's or the user's needs.

■ Prioritization - the process of determining the priority of a task.

■ Product - general definition of the digital product. A generalized concept that defines a dynamic product or service that is created in accordance with business requirements and user needs. It may refer to a website, web application, mobile application, watch application, service delivery system, etc.

■ Product Owner (PO) is a role in the Scrum team responsible for the project's outcome.

■ Prototype - the first full-scale or partial, but usually functional, form of a new product. It is used to test the initial design and reduce the cost of product development.

■ Rapport - a friendly, harmonious relationship characterized by agreement, mutual understanding, or empathy, which makes communication possible or easy. In business communication, "Rapport" is communication within the boundaries of subordination between roles, but in a friendly and easy way.

■ Release - an action related to creating an application, website, or other product for users.

■ The release candidate is a software version that usually does not have a final form. Although the version is functional, it is not ready for sale to the general public. In the Scrum methodology, a release candidate is a fragment of a product (feature or version) that extends an existing product and is prepared during a sprint (2-4 weeks).

■ Roadmap - a road map of the product that determines its development path.

■ Scope - scope of tasks or topics that need to be worked out to create a product.

■ Stakeholder - a representative or member of the client's team with information or knowledge that can be applied to create a product. Someone who: advises, approves, advocates, informs or constrains the development team.

■ Storytelling is an approach used to describe a particular situation, problem, or artifact to give your story a basic structure and engage your audience. Using this method, you fully reveal the story using storytelling techniques - connecting all the pieces logically and moving from the problem to the solution.

■ Usability measures how well a specific user in a particular context can use the product/design to achieve a defined goal effectively, efficiently, and quickly.

Printed in Great Britain
by Amazon